CONTENTS

Preface vii

John Lee 1

Ken Richardson 35

Robert J. Ackerman 71

Terry Kellogg 95

Mike Lew 125

Pat Mellody 153

Resource List 191

But life shakes like a drum and would discover resonances of what it loves in its own beat, the old man wetting and heating the head of the drum until it answered the tone he sought that sought him.

Robert Duncan
from *Bending the Bow*

the denial of our pain
our unwillingness to enter wholly
into the moment
leaves us like someone
trying to pick fruit
in the midst of a burning orchard

Steven Levine
from *Healing into Life and Death*

A dunce once searched for a fire with a lighted lantern
Had he known what fire was,
He could have cooked his rice much sooner.

Mu-mon, *The Gateless Gate*, A.D. 1228
from Paul Reps, *Zen Flesh, Zen Bones*

DEDICATION

To my sons, Daniel and Peter
May the choices be theirs
and
To my daughter, Julia
That she may understand.

ACKNOWLEDGMENTS

I want first to thank the six men who shared their wisdom, their experience and their brotherhood with me in creating this book. Their generosity of spirit made it possible for me to do this work and to offer it to our brothers and sisters.

My gratitude goes to Paul Jacobsen, who accompanied me in the journey of writing this book. His constant feedback helped me to see the book as others might. I am also extremely grateful to Binnie Ross for her support and feedback throughout the whole project. Ty Menefee cannot go unmentioned for his constant, quiet strength. I also want to remember Dr. Pat Stainbrook who was there when the door cracked open.

Finally, I am extremely grateful to Ann Eisler for her help in the final editing stages. Her selflessness in taking on a large project in the midst of a busy schedule made this a much better book. I am also grateful to her for pointing out that women who are concerned with how men see themselves may learn from what these six men have shared.

PREFACE

Men Speak Out emerged out of my own recovery process and my journey into the conscious men's movement. My debt to Robert Bly's work is enormous. Without his seminal exploration of myth to define man's journey, this book would not have been possible. I am equally indebted to the pioneering work in the exploration of the self that has been carried on by the six men who chose to be interviewed.

In the course of following these two trails to come to a more visceral understanding of myself, I came to find my heart. I had denied having one until it broke down at the age of 49. As I recuperated from that attack, I came to understand that I had lived a life of denial and that I had minimized and ignored my true feelings of self.

I am grateful to the spirituality of 12-Step programs and the conscious men's movement for helping me to find a direction. Most of all, I'm grateful for their help in acknowledging the heart of a man. My curiosity and (to a lesser extent) my training as a research scholar led me to read widely in the field of addiction recovery and co-dependency. I could not avoid the observation in the late 1980s that most of the new books on self-analysis had been written for, by and about women. I knew from my own experience starting in 1987 that men might comprise one in four or even one in ten in various self-help groups.

By 1989 our numbers had grown. At the first conference on "Men, Relationships and Co-dependency" held in Phoenix in 1990, 400 men and 75 women recognized publicly that recovery from co-dependency was a man's issue as well. This book started at that conference with the strong support of John Lee and Ken Richardson, who were the co-chairmen. By then it was clear to me that I wanted to do a book about men's consciousness and men's recovery that was for, by and about men. That desire led to the creation of this book.

At that conference two simple and startling concepts came clear to me. The first was that it was all right to be a man and to explore a range of feelings that extended beyond anger, lust and denial. It was truly remarkable to be in the company of 400 men who were expanding their emotional horizons to the gentle and the noble. The second concept came clear at the closing ceremony where men over 50 were celebrated as elders of the tribe. The younger men and women celebrated the older men simply for having survived to that point. In turn, the older men were encouraged to mentor the younger members of the tribe. It was extraordinary to participate in a ceremony that broke through the divisions of age that usually separate us.

Men Speak Out is composed of interviews with six men who have been instrumental in the definition and treatment of co-dependency, that complex of emotional dysfunctions and addictive behaviors that results from childhood abuse and abandonment. For some time the public has accepted the notion that co-dependency is a "woman's disease." This misapprehension stems from the original diagnosis of "co-alcoholism" as a set of emotional problems experienced by wives of alcoholic men.

As our understanding of co-dependency has developed through the pioneering work of Terry Kellogg, Pat and Pia Mellody and others, we have come to understand that this "cunning and baffling" disease applies to a broad range of people. More importantly, we have learned that it is distinct from addiction to any one substance or behavior.

The phenomenal growth of CoDA (Co-Dependents Anonymous) to include more than 100,000 people in the United States alone over a five-year period constitutes dramatic statistical evidence of the expanded concept of recovery from the disease. Perhaps the most surprising connection from a clinical standpoint has been the supportive relationship established between the emerging men's consciousness movement and work with co-dependency.

The Purpose

The primary purpose of *Men Speak Out* is to explore the core issues that are present in men's hearts. My starting point began with one question that underlay the whole list I presented to the interviewees: "How does recovery from the disease of co-dependency define men's lives?" This one question opened discussion on a whole series of issues. At the conference, Shepherd Bliss explored the idea that men are raised as "work objects," and that term grounded discussions about the place of work in a man's life.

John Lee introduced the idea that it was of central importance for a man to be able to grieve his losses. Again and again he emphasized the importance of grieving in becoming free of the past so one could become his true self and his best self.

To take the lid off those three concepts — aging, work and grieving — is to release a huge amount of male energy. Women had been given the job of mirroring and carrying men's feelings. The energy released in reclaiming these three topics with the support of the conscious men's movement gives men the opportunity to explore and re-possess their own feelings. The freedom and independence inherent in this work is breathtaking. We may or may not come to inhabit the same emotional landscape as before, but whatever that territory looks like it will be authentically our own. We are coming to discover that masculinity need not be toxic, and we are revealing that fact in our own way.

The Technique

I chose the technique of documentary interviewing for print as it was developed by Studs Terkel in *Division Street America*, *Working* and other books, and as it has been modeled by Bill Moyers in many of his TV interviews. I remembered long years ago when I lived in Chicago that Studs taught me that the Halsted Street bus was my University of Chicago. Studs has always known how to evoke what was authentic in people's experience. Bill Moyers has that same capacity with an entirely different style. My intention has been to honor their approach and their honesty about the human condition.

The six men I interviewed have made a difference in our perception of conscious men and in the way we live our lives as men in late 20th century America. As a writer, I thought it would be more valid, more real — more authentic, finally — for the reader to be able to listen to the voices of these six men who have been instrumental in changing men's understanding of their being and their role.

Each person is distinct in his issues and his focus. Yet each interview was conducted from the same menu of subjects and questions. In this respect the canons of obtaining and recording oral history (as well as basic anthropological practice) were observed in using "a standard instrument" which each person could respond to.

The structure of the book allows the reader to open it at random and read any one interview. From there you may move to any other interview, or you may consult the endnotes or the resource list to continue exploration of themes opened in the interviews.

The Men And Their Topics

The degree of difference in the tone and subject matter of the responses is perhaps surprising. Mike Lew, who has done ground-breaking work with men recovering from childhood sexual abuse; Terry Kellogg, who is a critically important worker behind the scenes; and Bob

Ackerman, a significantly important researcher, all had agendas of their own that happened to (more or less) coincide with the menu of questions. The other people used "the instrument" as a springboard to expand on their experiences and their conclusions. The result is a surprising variety of opinions at the same time that a unanimity of perception occurs.

Conclusion

Through co-dependency work and the conscious men's movement, we have come to understand that it is men's business to support each other and to provide an environment where we can grieve our losses. It is uniformly agreed by the interviewees of this book that the ability to grieve is requisite to finding our true selves. How this work is done will vary for every man, yet no one denies that it must be done by all.

It is only through grieving that we will achieve the space to be our true selves. Hopefully, these interviews will give people the models and the examination of roles, particularly work roles, to aid them in their journeys toward awareness and healing the self.

JOHN LEE

JOHN LEE

John Lee is known for his personal warmth, energy and integrity in his work with men. John's teaching experiences began in 1978 at Austin Community College in Austin, Texas. He chose Austin as his home and there founded the Austin Men's Center, which he still directs. He also has taught religion and American studies at the Universities of Texas and Alabama.

He brings this wide background to his private practice, which specializes in men's issues, co-dependency, addictive relationships and adult children of dysfunctional families. In addition to his private practice, John is well-known publicly for his three books, *The Flying Boy: Healing the Wounded Man; Flying Boy II: I Don't Want to be Alone: A Journey through Co-dependency and Addictive Relationships,* and *Recovery: Plain and Simple.*

John maintains an intense schedule of workshops around the country that range from his work at conferences and other professional settings to his well-known

"Wildman Gatherings," where over 100 men meet in rural settings from the Ocate wilderness in northern New Mexico to the hills of Texas or North Carolina. The gatherings create a communal setting through drumming, ritual, open fires and work with mythopoetic sources for men to recognize, own and share their deepest feelings.

Gatherings such as these are rare in this culture because they provide opportunities for men to bond and share with each other in non-competitive, non-threatening social environments. One of John's most important principles is that each man learns to define his masculinity through his ability to grieve the losses of his past, just as he learns another aspect of his masculinity by his ability to wield a metaphorical sword or by knowing when to rest and when to work.

John's work has centered on grappling with a number of issues that have unique characteristics as they are experienced by men. These issues include:

Dysfunctional or non-existent relationships with the father
Inappropriate bonding with the mother
Overly "dramatic" lifestyle
Inability to commit to jobs or people
Workaholic tendencies
Rigid body structure
History of drug or alcohol use
Need for control
Lack of spontaneity
Inability to express anger appropriately.

In order to fully inhabit our true selves, we need to break free from the past, from the internalized controls of our major caregivers. We need also to experience "soul," which John evokes as an activated presence of spirit within the body. He observes that many men reside only in their heads, only on their spirit sides or only in their bodies — but that the real task is to bring all three elements together in the present. Recovery for John involves the reintegration of body and spirit into soul.

John's work in all of these settings recognizes that most men need the support of other men as they work to discover their true selves. At a particular stage of a man's recovery, he needs to work without the presence of women to be able to find himself. That time is the time of the Wildman. The term Wildman derives from Robert Bly's interpretation of the "Iron John" myth by the Brothers Grimm. John's use of this myth and others points to his relationship with Bly's mythopoetic men's movement.

John and I met in the summer of 1990 in the garden of a home in Santa Fe, New Mexico. I had just experienced a Wildman Gathering conducted by John and his partner Marvin Allen in the Ocate wilderness east of Taos, New Mexico. The bonding of that intense weekend carried us into the interview that follows.

INTERVIEW WITH
JOHN LEE

July 23, 1990 • Santa Fe, New Mexico

David Lenfest: Our subject is men's path, or how a man's life path is redefined by the men's movement and by the co-dependency movement. I'd like to start with an idea that Robert Bly[1] uses a lot — that of man's role as a hunter. Do you see yourself as a hunter in what you do?

John Lee: Men that we're working with are hunters, but because of the urbanization and the high technology that we live in, we've had to shift our mode of hunting to spirituality, hunting food for the spirit and sustenance for the soul. In that way I see myself as a hunter, and I see all the men that are involved with me still as hunters. We're stalking something savage, something wild, something wonderful, but it's food for the soul that we're seeking now.

David: What I get out of that metaphor is that we're hunting a sense of balance, a sense of beauty, almost in the Navajo way of saying "Walk in beauty." We're trying to learn how to walk in beauty.

John: Yeah, and I think one of the things that most men are willing to do now is deal with the ugly in every place that they find it in order to beautify their journey. They're really ready now to look at the ugly. They're ready to look at their addictions. They're ready to look at their dysfunctions. They're ready to look at their behaviors that are so patterned they can't heal.

David: Men are making a major effort to rid themselves of addictions of all kinds. I've been particularly interested in the addiction to work. In my own life, I've realized how addicted to work I have been. The contrast that comes up for me is the one between an addiction to work in order to rise up the ladder or just to satisfy the work habit, and a notion of right livelihood. I wonder how you feel about that difference?

John: I've been addressing my work addiction for a long time, particularly this last year. One cannot, man or woman, find their soul if they're trying to find it through work. Work is only a piece of the pie. In our culture, most people find their identity, their livelihood, their ego gratification through work. An attachment to work is actually an impediment to men finding their souls and dealing with their addictions. Work becomes an addiction by itself so you are constantly in this little rat's maze looking for yourself.

One of the reasons why most men are so scared to stop working is that if they do, they will start getting in touch with their soul and in touch with their pain. So they make excuses and find reasons to work all the time. If you took a man and told him he could only work 20 hours a week, all his stuff would come up because he would have time to look at it. If you tell a man that he has to work 40 or 50 or 60 hours a week, he's got plenty of time to avoid *everything*.

That's why the primitive hunting and gathering societies were said to have only worked an average of three hours a day to accumulate the food supplies they needed to sustain them. Now that we've got all this technology, we have to work overtime to pay for it. We're paying for it in more ways than one, in that we don't get to do the soul work. The Australian Aborigine is said to spend 60 to 70 percent of his day in spiritual, soul work. We do maybe two percent a week if we're lucky.

David: Do you think the Aboriginals have set a mark for us, a direction we should go?

John: No, because given the cultural context they find themselves in and the one we find ourselves in, there has to be a balance. We can't go back to primitive times. But we could do a number of things that would give us more time to be with ourselves and to be with the voices and the visions that we have latent, lying around loose in us.

But to do that you have to be working on yourself. You have to be working on your co-dependency and how much you depend upon your work to give you the stuff you say you need. I mean, do we need a house that costs $200,000? I don't think so. Do we need cars that cost $25,000 each? I don't think so. But, at the same time, there is a certain level of comfort that most of us desire after we get past 25. But for me a lot of it really is around healing co-dependency and not being so dependent on work.

David: Well, I see a path in this. I'm hearing you talk about a path in it as well, a path in which the first step is clearing up the addictions or getting into a place where they're manageable. As Pat Mellody says, once you've cleared away the addiction to alcohol, you're ready to face up to the co-dependency problems that underlie the alcohol addiction. I think that once you begin to get the co-dependency problems in line, then you begin to see your spiritual place and the place of the spirit in your everyday life.

John: That's right. And it's important to say that everything you just described is about a 50-year process. That
is the thing that not enough people talk about as far as I'm
concerned. The way we use language implies that it would
only take a little while to clear up our addictions. The way
we use our language also implies that once we clear up
our addictions we can get on with our spiritual quest.

The truth is, for me, that the clearing up of these addictions really is a life-long process. I don't know anyone who
is finished, but I do know some people who think they
are. I don't try to hang around with those people very
much because they scare me.

David: How do they scare you?

John: Well, either they have attained something that's
closer to sainthood than I can readily be comfortable with,
or they're in denial. Either one of those will frighten me.
A man in denial is scary. When I'm in my denial, I scare
people. I bring up old stuff for them. And when I see
somebody else in denial, it does it to me as well.

I mean, how many hours could you sit in the room with
the Dalai Lama? It would be very uncomfortable for me.
I'm not far enough along to be in the presence for very
long of anyone who feels like he's cleared up his addictions.
I've still got a bunch of 'em to work on, and I don't even
know what most of 'em are at this point.

David: In a way, that leads us around to something you
have written about in such exquisite detail. It's the question of how your own life has played into your own views.
I think that's really there in all of your books?

John: Right. One man said I have created a whole system of psychology on the case history of one. (Laughs.) I
think it's both a compliment and a criticism. And I'll accept
the good. I see the point. It's true that my work really is
based on my experience. I like to be with people who
share their experience and factual information. I love it.

But I really am just not called on that path. I've written about my experience and then tried to capture some of the experiences of the men who have worked with me. What we've found over the years is that *The Flying Boy* is a universal experience, but it doesn't apply to all. I have a partner in Austin who read *The Flying Boy* and said he didn't relate to it whatsoever.

But there's a lot about what's going on in my life that people relate to. I really try to draw upon a variety of sources — anthropology, primitive mythology, other cultures, Zen Buddhism, Taoism, gestalt, psychodrama — but I only study them as a way to heal myself. I don't study them as a way to get a whole bunch of facts about those systems to go out and tell people about those facts. I take 'em, run 'em through me and then tell my experience of those facts. That's very different.

David: Well, I think that sort of personal approach is one that many people apply in their own lives. I think many people — if they're honest with themselves — read stuff from Zen Buddhism or Vipassana or the life of Christ or what-have-you because they're looking for answers for themselves. I see you as simply being more honest than most.

John: Well, thank you. I've had a number of people say they wish there were more books written like *The Flying Boy*. Most of the books I read are written like the person has taken facts and integrated them into their life, and *now* they don't have any more problems.

That always disturbs me because it leaves me feeling "less than." So when I hear certain speakers, particularly in the men's movement or the recovery movement, give day-long workshops, I walk away going, "Damn, I wish I could be that healed." I feel like a lot of men do, too.

That approach sets up an artificial barrier between the listener and the speaker. More than that, I think it does some distinct soul damage because it puts the listener in the role of a child who will some day, with the help and grace of God, and listening to more people like this guy talking, get to be like this guy. And that's very, very dangerous to me. It's very dangerous. It's more dangerous than I've probably ever tried to articulate before.

David: That's interesting. So you don't want people to be like you?

John: Right. I would like very much for people to find things about what I say that they can use in their lives, but I'm more interested in me being like me as much as possible in front of as many people as possible — as opposed to being an authority or that kind of thing. That's just my personal preference.

David: Measuring ourselves seems to be part of the question that's implicit.

John: That's right, that's right.

David: In that respect, one of the questions I have is: do you think that the wildman or the trickster or the coyote figure in some way helps us to measure ourselves or see ourselves?

John: Well, all those are different archetypal energies that I believe are found in every human being, though each of those energies may manifest itself to greater or lesser degree depending on the person and that person's life cycle. For instance, at 60 I might have more trickster in me than I will wildman. And then at 70 the wildman may re-emerge more prominently than the trickster. I think part of the service of the mythopoetic movement is to bring men more fully in touch with those energies that are running through our psyches and through our souls. If we can call on that, and one of the ways we can is through our dreams, then that will help us heal in many ways because all those energies are available.

David: Do you think that, for a man, the break with the mother is similar to the break with his addictions?

John: That's a very interesting question.

David: I meet many men in this movement, men who are professionals, who continue to think of their mothers very fondly and almost never say anything critical about their mother at all. It's as if she remains venerated and a semi-Holy Virgin-type figure. I meet very few men who express anger with their mothers, while I meet lots who express and work out anger with their fathers. That's very curious to me.

John: That's a very good point. You're right that most men don't break with their mothers. But most men hate their mothers because their mothers did not teach them to break or inspire the separation. Therefore, most men hate their mothers so much that they can't ever get to it, because they're afraid that if they did, it would denigrate her memory if she's dead, or their present mother if she's alive.

One of the things that I make a distinction about in my work is that if men would deal with their ghost mother and deal with their ghost father, they would be able to make that break. And — I hadn't quite thought about it until you framed it that way — one of the reasons why they have to do addictions, one of the many reasons, is because they can't realize that they're still in the force field of the mother.

If you knock back a pint of whiskey, you can forget that you didn't make the break. If you drink a pint of whiskey, you can forget that you haven't separated from the father either. A functional father and mother would have, through a number and series of behaviors and statements and actions, perpetuated a clean break with the son and daughter. Since we don't have any of those functional folks looming around to show us how, we really don't know much about it. But parents who cannot let go of their children rear children who turn into adults who can't let go of their parents.

David: To me, so much of the recovery program and the men's movement has to do with individuation, with our becoming individuals, becoming free from the bottle, whether it's the bottle with the nipple on it or the bottle of booze, free from the addiction to work. And that also means becoming free from parents, which is what underlies this question. You're quite right, it takes a long time. It may take 40 or 50 years for a man to get to the place where he's ready to break free of all that and not be hooked in.

John: The problem is that our culture does not very often teach you that it's okay to kill your parents. Freud and Nietzsche both said that a man has to kill the father. Everybody knows that, but nobody knows what that means. The ones who knew what it meant didn't want to do it because until a man kills his father and his mother he can't re-parent himself. He keeps those negative introjected voices in the back of his head, where his crown is, that speak down to him early in the morning hours saying things like, "Get up out of bed, you lazy son of a bitch, and go on and get to work." That's the negative introjected father in there.

I have a tape, *Saying Goodbye to Mom and Dad,* and I have an exercise I do in my day-long workshops of saying goodbye to Mom and Dad. The house will be in tears and snot the moment that exercise is set up because it's one of the most painful events of our entire lifetime. When we can't do it, we stay children, we stay counter-productive, we stay less than creative.

It's really a major, major task to be accomplished, and yet it's one that most people are scared of. Here's one of the reasons why. If a man barely knew his father because his father was emotionally or physically absent, and then you tell that man he's got to kill off what little he's got, he sinks into depression for a while, he sinks into terror for a while, and he gets pissed off at the person who tells him that's what he needs to do, given that he never had a father to begin with.

So there's this fine, very fine silk thread that connects him and his father. Then at a workshop I'll say, "We have to let our father go." And the guy goes, "But then I'll just float away. If I let my mom go, I'll just float away." And what I've said is "No, what will happen is that fine silk thread will turn into this huge golden rope that will connect you to the archetypal father and to the positive introjected father you have inside you." And then, if your mother and father are still alive in the present moment, then you might even be able to have a reasonably healthy relationship with them. That's the benefit of all of this.

David: So part of this process we're talking about is that the negative images of both mother and father are being replaced through work in the program, work in the movement, by healthy archetypal images, and the connection into these archetypes is Jungian.

John: Very much so. Now what we try to do in the 12-Step programs and in the men's gatherings is that we don't talk a lot of Jungian stuff, we try to do it. One of the things I'm working on now is a book on Jung for recovering people. I don't know what it's going to be called yet, but it's already sort of in the works. I really feel it's time to make explicit some of the Jungian ideas that a lot of us are operating with and just not calling. So, it will take people who are in recovery a step deeper because Jungian stuff is really deep. I think it will help some folks out, particularly dealing with anima and animus stuff.

David: Well, I find Robert Moore[3] very interesting to listen to, but I'm sure there are lots of people around who, when Moore talks about the warrior, talks about the king, talks about the lover, can't plug that theory into behavior patterns. You're up to making those connections?

John: That's right. At least I want to for the next 20 years or so. I read Robert Moore and listen to his tapes, and I think it works very well for a certain type of individual — the academic, the intellectual. But my work has never really been geared for the academic and intellectual. My work has been geared more for people like me. Even though I have an academic and intellectual background and a strong bent toward that, I also have my roots firmly planted in the hills of Alabama and the prairies of Texas. Those are the men I feel must be reached, and the ideas that somebody like Moore articulates so eloquently go way over most of those guys' heads.

What I want to do and have always wanted to do is to make this stuff concrete, physical, bodily and simple because there's more of those guys than there are academic and intellectual men. And that doesn't take anything away from Moore. It simply says that his work is for one group of folks, mine is for another. And maybe, yes, my audience might be a little bit larger because I really want to go to the guy who's pushing that bulldozer over there and give him some tools to work with.

David: Right. Let me shift the focus just slightly. I think this is really interesting stuff, and I want to pursue another line. Did you have a male initiation, and can you describe it if you had one? What was it like?

John: I've never had that question asked of me before, so I've never given it much thought, but the initiation that I feel was very symbolic . . . In 1981, when the interview came out with Robert Bly from Keith Thompson in *New Age*[4] I read that. And after that I read everything that Bly had to teach and say. Everywhere. I got all his tapes. Couldn't go to his gatherings at the time because I didn't have any money, but I got familiar with it.

It was like the initial stages or the beginnings of an initiation. When Laurel (in *The Flying Boy*) left me, I went into grief unlike I'd ever been into before or since. I went into that grief every day for nine months — getting up in the mornings, weeping, writing, howling, screaming, the whole thing, every day (except for eight days according to my journal) for nine months. For me, I see that as the almost full-blown initiation process.

By the time I got out of that, I literally said, "I'm going to start working with men now." I didn't say that consciously by saying "I've been initiated now." I didn't think that at all. But looking back to five years ago when I started my first men's group, one of the first men's groups in Austin, I can see that the reason I felt I had that right was because of what I had just come through.

The reason why I had that right is because I had to some degree actualized and embodied a lot of what Bly had been writing and saying through that grieving process. And while five years later I still have not assimilated or actualized maybe even one-tenth of what he has been talking about, I did enough for me to get started on the path with the men's group and gatherings and those kinds of things.

David: We were talking about the Wildman Weekend that just took place outside Taos in July. I found it empowering to be placed in the circle of elders 50 and over. In a way, it justified a lot of experiences I had gone through that I thought had just been trashed and were behind me. Because it's my sense as a 54-year-old man with three careers behind me that there's been a lot of wastage in my life. Being inducted into the circle of elders told me that not all was wasted.

John: Not a goddamned ounce. It's like one man said one time at a gathering. He was crying and said, "I don't deserve to be here." He said, "I've wasted so much of my life that I don't deserve to be here." Then he just paused for a moment and said, "But come to think of it, I've gone through some deaths, I've gone through a bankruptcy, I've cleaned up from alcoholism and drug abuse. I've put two kids through school and one through college. I buried my father. Maybe I do deserve to be here. I survived all those things."

I think that's really what it says in that circle. See, one of the things I've always believed, and I've never said it in public, is that everything we do has at the center of it, no matter how self-destructive it appears, a distinct speck of light that is moving us toward wholeness and individuation. So I look at all the self-destructive behavior in my relationship with Laurel, and yet . . . I'll give you a more concrete example.

There was a period of time when if you asked me exactly what it would take to get Laurel back, I knew the answer. I knew what it would take. I did the opposite because there was something in me that knew more than I. There are people who would say that if you know what it would take and you keep doing this, you're just self-destructive. But in the middle of that self-destructive behavior was a speck of knowing that could not be identified or seen or spoken of, that knew if I had done what it took I wouldn't be where I am now.

David: You would have been going backwards.

John: That's right. And there was a speck in me that knew that. But yet if it was observed by outside people, they'd say, "He's just being self-destructive as hell. He loves this woman and if he would just do A, B and C, he'd probably get her back." And I was doing D, E and F.

David: You couldn't have been true to yourself doing A, B and C.

John: That's right. When a man says, "I've had two divorces, I've wasted my life," and he's sitting in a men's gathering, I know and something in him knows that it took exactly those two divorces to get him right where he's at. And where he's at now is in some total way more healthy and healing and vulnerable than if he had stayed in one of those marriages. And he knows it.

What that means is that implicit in every act of self-destruction is a movement toward growth. People could think that's a very dangerous idea.

David: It is a dangerous idea.

You're interested in the body and the movement of the body. Maybe you can tell us how you see recapturing the body? I know for myself that I've done several kinds of physical disciplines. Each time I take one up I feel a lot better about myself.

John: You see, that's what I wanted to point out. In the recovery movement and in some aspects of the men's movement, the body is not activated. The body is not enlivened by the process. So much of recovery is about information. It's about speaking and talking. And the men's movement, a large part of it, is about information and speaking and talking. Those are absolutely necessary and absolutely valuable, but the contribution that I want to make, which is not unique to me, is my interest in the body. I think it's very much neglected in the recovery movement and in the men's movement.

David: I think the only recognition people give is that as people work through stuff, they have body memories. And so the body memories are used to access incest issues or earlier kinds of childhood abuse issues. But they don't see that you have to keep squeezing — it's almost as if the body is an emotional sponge, and you have to wring that thing out with regularity if you're going to keep working.

John: That's right, that's right. The body is, to try to paraphrase those who have already written about it like Louwen and others, a charge-building system. And if the body is not discharged on a regular basis, then in my opinion it will help cause disease and other addictions to keep you from remembering. And that's a very interesting word for me, re-membering the body. If I drink enough, I can forget I have a body. If I work enough, I can forget I have a body. So earlier we were talking about finding the soul. One of the ways, I believe, to find the soul is through the vehicle and through the pathway of the body. Indeed, for me it's almost like the soul lives in the body.

I trace that back and look at a couple of cultures, the Caucasian culture and the Black American culture. When they talk about soul and they talk about that aspect of their life, they're always talking about the body. There's soul food and there's soul music. And it goes in and it is expressed through the body. The spirit, on the other hand, is something more ethereal, more high and elevated.

So what I want to do is bring that body and soul aspect back. I believe that most of the men I work with, whether in recovery or in the men's gatherings, have a strong connection to their spirits. Their spiritual lives are not that shabby, but their soulful lives are almost totally neglected. I define soul as in union with body, as the body is the container of the soul. So, therefore, it's like most of us are very spiritual, but not very soulful. In many times, in other cultures you will see a lot of soul, but not very much spirit. And so what I'm hoping for in my own personal life is more of a combining of those two, doing things like prayer and meditation for my spirit, doing things like dancing, drumming, pounding a pillow with a bat for my soul. The total container that I am is the house for both, but they're not the same thing.

David: This weekend it occurred to me that the spirit of Wilhelm Reich[5] must be just exultant over what's going on because we're seeing a lot of stuff that he was writing about in the '40s and early '50s — and was sent to jail for — becoming emblazoned across America.

John: Right. That's right. Reich is very much an influence, but more so as he was translated and influenced by Alexander Louwen. For me, I could never read Reich very well because he was so intellectual and so hard to follow. But I certainly read some of him, and I know this. I use a lot of Reichian, bio-energetic stuff in my own therapy practice and in my own daily life. I do bio-energetic exercises in the morning to get the energy moving up and down my body. Yoga and those kinds of things are very useful for that. Tai Chi as well.

The problem that I've experienced with Tai Chi and Yoga is the same problem I see with people who run and lift weights. Many people, men particularly, do all those endeavors with their mind. They don't do them with their bodies. You can watch very often the face of a man who runs, for instance, or the face of a man who does Yoga, and most of his energy will be concentrated from his eyes up. Indeed, sometimes in his jaws. And he'll be running from here up. He's got to run three miles so he's focused, he's concentrated. And the same thing with Yoga. I've seen Yoga and Tai Chi literally carried out in some people from the neck up, and it's the most amazing thing to watch. They still haven't translated that ancient art into the body. And a good teacher will recognize that, but sometimes it'll get past them.

So the body is very, very much an integral part of recovery, it's an integral part of the men's movement, and yet it's one that's being omitted. I try to address that in my training program for counselors. Maybe it's time to resurrect Reich and put him to work.

David: I think that's in fact happened, but the straight medical model is strictly in a person's head, and it doesn't look at a synthetic process going on — a body/mind process. I was thinking of Ken Dychtwald's book, *Body/Mind,*[6] from a few years ago, which creates a whole construct there in language that we can get to when otherwise the language is pretty arcane.

John: That book is one of the best. You know, the interesting thing is that everybody's read it, but they never really brought it into their practice. They'd say, "Yes, he's right," and then they would sit in their offices and say things to their clients like, "Oh, you're angry. Tell me more about that." And I go, "Didn't you read Ken Dychtwald's book? Didn't you read Alexander Louwen? What do you mean, tell you more about that, man? I've got a charge on that is the size of this house. How am I going to discharge that energy around my father by *telling* you about it?"

The truth is it does help. It does work a little bit, but mixing that with the actual physical expression of it will help. To the point, I was speaking with one of my colleagues the other day, and he said that he likes to just say things right out when he feels them and get it out. And what he does in some ways, in my opinion, is discharge the energy around it.

But just saying it is to me a less effective way of dealing with it than discharging it through a very physical bodily way and then, once the energy has dissipated, saying what's left. For instance, if I get angry at you, my premise is (and has been for years) that probably, if I'm super charged up about it, it has less to do with you and more to do with me and my history. If I'm just moderately charged and my body's not all cranked up and in knots, then it might just be about me and you. But if I'm really scared and I'm really twisted and I'm really hyped up, it's almost guaranteed to have more to do with something about me and my mom or me and my dad than it does about me and you, because no you in the present could have that kind of effect over this me in the present. So it must be kicking off something from back there.

So what I've taught for years is for you to take that, then, and discharge it in a way other than blowing me out of the chair with it. You discharge it in a way to separate — by using the body — what is Mom and Dad when you were five years old from what is just me and you. Then I can hear what is me and you won't blow me out of the water and put all your old stuff on me.

David: It's exactly the same process that says if I have a rage attack over a particular event, it's probably not my present anger. It's carried anger from one of my major caregivers that's finding expression because it's been triggered by some event in the present. So my real job is to connect that up, see it and discharge it in order to be clear about dealing with the present, so I'm not infecting it with all that unresolved crap in the background.

John: That's right. The problem with a lot of it is that people try to do it intellectually, and it's not intellectual. That's why I use the body. The body is pre-verbal. The mind is verbal. If we're in an altercation and there is all that tremendous charge, and if I don't move it out of my body in some way, I'll try to move it out of my body verbally and onto your body because it's got to get out.

David: Well, that gets us around to dignity — real dignity and false dignity. A question I have goes like this, "Is there dignity in handling pain, and is that different from old-fashioned stoicism?"

John: There is dignity in handling pain. Stoicism, for me, is another more subtle form of self-pity. Stoicism and self-pity are almost kissing cousins for me. If I have pain, no matter how big the pain is, if I grieve that pain out, it only takes moments in the scheme of things.

Stoicism takes lifetimes to master. Self-pity is a waste of lifetimes. Grief is the most dignified act that one can perform if it's separated from self-pity. A lot of people don't know the difference.

David: How do we distinguish between the two?

John: Well, let me just give you some down-home examples. A man gets a divorce from his wife. There is self-pity if she leaves him. He goes and gets drunk and he doesn't shave and he doesn't take a bath and he doesn't eat very well. He goes and punches the jukebox full of quarters and that tells him his baby left him and he ain't worth a shit because of it. That's self-pity.

The same man who is willing to be dignified will call another man and say, "My wife left me. I know you know about such things. I'd like to come over and stay with you for a couple of days. I'd like to talk with you, and I'd like for you to hold me. I'd like you to listen to me cry, and I'd like for you to watch me beat the shit out of this pillow until I just can't beat it any more. And while I'm doing that, I would like for you to prepare me three good meals a day."

And then for weeks he would write and he would cry and he would journal and he would go to a men's support group. He'd cry and he'd journal and he'd beat and he'd journal. He'd keep doing that. And all the time, though, he would be eating, exercising, getting support. That is dignity. That is grief. And that is something very, very different from self-pity. And within three to six months time max, no matter how important that woman was, he would be through 80, maybe only 75 percent of all the grief work he would need around that particular issue.

Now, if he has never grieved before and she leaves him, then all of the grief of relationships past including that of the mother and father will come rushing out, so it will take longer. But most men in their self-pity or their stoicism will simply go get another woman. Or they will throw themselves into 70-hour work weeks. Or they will go buy themselves a new car. And they'll keep a stiff upper lip. Yet they will never tap into the thing that would really restore their dignity and, to some degree, deepen their masculinity.

David: We've been tossing around the term "masculinity," and sometimes we've talked about it as deep and sometimes as shallow. I wonder what we can say toward defining the term?

John: Masculinity? You know, my partner, Marvin Allen, director of the Men's Center, talks about creative masculinity, and I really like that notion a lot. Basically, what he means is that each individual man creates his own definition of what is masculine. I credit him for that.

True, deep masculinity is a man who knows when to wield a metaphorical sword and when to sheathe it, when to grieve and when to get angry, when to rest and when to work, when to nurture and when to receive nurturing.

Basically, the masculine man is the one who knows how to grieve. If he doesn't know how to grieve and he's not willing to participate in that act as often as necessary, then there is something about his masculinity that has yet to be formed.

David: What about taking joy in something as the obverse of the coin of grieving? We don't talk about that very much.

John: Well, that's because we don't talk about grief. A man who cannot grieve cannot experience joy. And most men can't grieve, so there's not a whole lot of joy to be discussed in this culture. Yes, it's out there. Yes, it's available. And yes, over the past few years I've experienced quite a bit of it. More and more all the time. But I watch myself from week to week, and the weeks I shut down my body and my soul from grieving are the same weeks I don't feel that happy either.

They are so integrally related that we have to first discuss grief and then joy. After that nine months of grieving for Laurel, I have to tell you, man, I was ecstatic. And then for a while, another level of grief came up. I went into it, and the joy came up again. It's been that cycle consistently.

David: Do you think a majority of males in this culture are raised by women to be naive? And consequently, that it takes betrayal to awaken them into fully realized anger?

John: Well, I believe that most males are raised to be naive. That's true. But not necessarily by women. The father, either through commission or omission, raises his son to be naive as well. You put that with a woman who is angry at the man and at men in general, and you're going to have a very naive son.

Naivete is one of the most subtle modes of being that the men's movement has yet to address, and the recovery movement has almost not addressed it at all.

David: The recovery movement has not addressed it at all?

John: I have never seen or heard in any discussion, any workshop or any book that I've read on recovery, about the whole idea of naivete in men or women. I think one of the reasons is, as we said earlier, some of the leading figures in the recovery field are still very naive themselves. The whole recovery business is a very naive business in many ways.

The whole recovery business is really built on the presupposition that you can teach anybody anything. You have to have a certain amount of idealism and naivete to even be in the recovery business or the men's movement or the college teaching profession. If you really believe that you can teach somebody anything, I think you're kind of naive.

I'm still a very naive male. I uncover it all the time in my work, particularly with other men. In projects or business deals I find myself terribly naive, but in my work I don't ever presuppose that I'm teaching anybody anything. That's why again I rely upon my personal experience. I really feel like I am a teacher, and a good teacher I think, but it's because I don't really believe that firmly in the act of teaching. I say, "Here's my experience. Does that draw anything out of you that you already know but maybe have forgotten?"

David: I think you also say, "I'm here to witness the process you're going through, to validate that process."

John: That's very different from teaching, very different from writing a book that says, "Go do what I did or what I tell you to do." That's naive to me, because nobody will do that. You know, you read these books on recovery and until you are slapped right up against the wall, you don't do hardly one-hundredth of what they say.

David: No, you remain a tourist in somebody else's reality.

John: That's right. So what I try to do, through experience, through the body in many ways, is to bring that person into their own reality by using my experience. The naive male believes that the uninitiated male, the male who is not in recovery, still has his best interest at heart — and he doesn't, I don't believe. The initiated male, the recovering male, is more apt to more of the time.

David: Again, I was using the term *naive* in somewhat the way Bly uses it, particularly in the story, "The Devil's Sooty Brother," where the fellow spends seven years underground firing the pots. So he spends seven years underground working on his own issues, and when the shavings turn into gold, he promptly gives them away.

John: That's naivete. That's the whole act of teaching in a way. Many of us, like myself, have taken years to get the gold we've finally got. I've given so much gold away, I barely have enough to buy any land. I just do that (Laughs.) because of my naivete.

David: I was thinking more of a figurative sense than a literal one.

John: That's what I mean. Teaching is a way of doing that. It's like I've worked real hard to get this, and then it's like that image — casting pearls out. That was one of the things about college teaching for me. I loved it. It should be an honored and revered profession. But there you are standing before 30 people and of that 30 people, in undergraduate school particularly, only three of them want to be there. And you're pouring your soul out as if . . .

David: . . . All 30 wanted to be there. That's why I quit.

John: And your gold is just dribbling right out. Now, luckily, those three would stick some in their pockets and that would make you feel good enough to do it year after year after year. But you really believed — most of us in our naivete really wanted to believe — that it was more like 27 or 28 who were getting it. But they really weren't. They really weren't. But at age 25 or 26, when you're teaching, you need to believe that stuff.

David: One of the things as 20th century males we grew up with was hearing about a code, almost a code of male honor, a military code or a Marine code. Whatever the label, there was an idea that we were supposed to keep a stiff upper lip, be strong, be able to endure all this stuff, be able to produce. All of those kinds of personality descriptors were ways to become heroes. If we would only do all of them, we would be heroic. "Like who?" we might have asked, but we didn't.
I wonder . . . Pat Mellody seems to think that attempting to follow that code leads to "lives of quiet desperation." I wonder if that's what a lot of this recovery work and men's movement work is trying to get rid of — that quiet desperation?

John: I think so. It's trying to restore the individuality that we all need and a sense of independence within some sort of interdependent sphere. And yet the 12-Step programs in their shadow side and the men's movement in its shadow side can be accused of creating another kind of code that will end up being just as detrimental as the one they're trying to escape.

David: Would you describe that shadow side?

John: Well, the shadow side of the men's movement projects the notion that the way the men's movement should go is the way that I say it should go, or the way Robert Bly

says it should go, or the way Shepherd Bliss says it should
go — and that if people don't agree with the way we say
it, then they're not in the men's movement. They're to be
somehow demeaned because . . .

David: They're not orthodox.

John: Right. And so rather than letting that shadow
swallow us, I say things like, "Look, do your work. Provide
men of the community with support by doing any kind of
men's group you want. It emerges out of your soul, not
mine or Shepherd's or Robert's or anybody else's." There
is a trace of unhealed egotism and competition in those of
us in the movement who kind of think we know the best
way to do it. If you really want to be in the men's movement, you do it our way. That's our shadow, you know.
And so that's one side.

The other side is that if the men's movement only
reaches the white, Anglo-Saxon, middle-American, 30- to
55-year-old man, we will have really embarrassed ourselves and hurt the planet at large. We will have formed
another type of country club or another type of Kiwanis
or Jaycees, and we don't need any more of those. A lot of
the men's movement stuff, as it is practiced by several
people, is for men who can pay me the money. And then
all you have is just another facet of the human potential,
new age growth movement. Neither of those is bad in a
way, but they're not going to take the movement as far as
we hope it will go, which includes cross-cultural and sexual and other things. That's a shadow side.

The shadow side of the recovery movement is the im-
plied notion that, even though the leaders of that movement say recovery is a process, many of them behave, act
and sound as if they've already acquired the product.
And that's what I was saying earlier. There is that separation of what Buber[7] talked about, an I and a Thou, or
an I and an It.

One time at a conference a man introduced himself as
a recovered co-dependent. And I went, "*Wow!*" He may be

but I don't want to listen to him. Because if he is, I don't
know what I have to learn from him because he's just too
far away from my experience. My experience says it's a
process. I'm going to be recovering. I'm going to slip into
and out of co-dependency, depending on circumstance and
people and how tired I am and how stressed out I am.
And if he's recovered . . . I saw in the audience, a very
large audience, heads turn and heard whispers, "Did he
say 'recovered'?"

I was the next person on, and I was very careful to say,
very slowly, "Hi, my name is John and I'm a recovering
co-dependent." Implicit in that was not a judgment on
him, but simply to say if this guy is recovered, that's
great, but I can't relate to him. So the dark side appears
when I'm in a 12-Step meeting and I never see any therapists. I never see the people at the meetings who, on
their cards or their brochures or whatever, state that
they specialize in co-dependency and addiction. I never
see them at any meetings.

Okay, maybe they don't need meetings. That's not for
me to judge. The point is that their clients do not see
them at meetings either. So there's this artificial thing set
up again that says, "I'll tell you to go to meetings, but
don't expect to see me there. I specialize in it, but I do
something else." What do you do? There's a real shadow
side in that for me. The other shadow side that's in the
men's movement and the co-dependency movement is to
jump on the bandwagon too quickly. The shadow side of
the men's movement is the same as the co-dependency
thing. Last year the psychotherapist specialized in couples
counseling and relationships. This year on his card he's
doing men's groups and men's gatherings and specializing
in men's issues. Ask him how he got from here to there so
quickly and sometimes the answer is very scary. "I went
to a men's gathering once. I saw Bill Moyers and Robert
Bly's interview." I mean, it's kind of scary.

David: See one, do one, teach one?

John: That's right. That's the shadow side right there. The same thing with co-dependency. Last month they weren't specializing in co-dependency. This month they are. Did you see them at meetings? Did you see them at Sierra Tucson[8]? No. They just decided they were specialists. Those are very dangerous shadow sides as well.

David: I think those people are always with us. They're the shadow side of the coyote, and any self-respecting Navajo will tell you the coyote is not a good figure. The coyote is not fun. But he's necessary and he's out there. It's just like the rattlesnake.

John: He lives. He keeps the other folks honest and calls them to task, to look at their shadow side. I have looked at my own shadow side. I've questioned what gives me the right to do this. Sometimes I don't have as good an answer as others.

David: I thank Pat Mellody for this question. Pat emphasized a notion from Maslow[9] that "a satisfied need is not a motivator." I hear somewhat the same thing from Thich Nhat Hanh[10], the Vietnamese Buddhist monk, when he talks about recognizing the good things in our lives, recognizing what he calls the "non-toothache." He asks us to compare how we feel when we don't have a toothache to how we feel when we do. And he refers to this as our "non-toothache." Recognize the blessings in our lives in this way, be those as simple as a glass of fresh water. And that comes up again in Maslow's more elaborated language.

So the question I'm directing at you really comes in terms of the men's movement and the way the men's movement has gone. Can we criticize the movement for generating needs and problems that aren't really there? Are we talking about a "non-toothache"? Are we talking about "satisfied needs"?

This is a very complicated way of asking, "Is this stuff real?" Is this going to have an impact in the real world of toothaches and the lower ranks of Maslow's need pyramid?

John: I don't know how this relates, but I'm thinking about it as you're saying this. Adult children who grew up in dysfunctional families have their whole system inverted so that the main motivator for an adult child is pain. When the adult child begins to move toward recovery, the system begins to realign itself into its proper place.

Let me give you an example from my own life. For years, I could not write unless I had experienced tremendous pain. I'd been taught through literature, through poetry, through my culture, that the only way one could accomplish work was through experiencing deep hurt and deep pain, and out of that, one gave birth to something positive and creative. I've been questioning that for years. Then recently I found myself writing a new book while I was in the happiest, healthiest relationship that I've ever been in.

I'm not writing this book out of pain, and according to my editors it's the best thing I've written so far. I hope they're right. When my girlfriend and I had a fight in the middle of the process of writing, I went into pain and I could no longer write. I haven't written a word since. Now I'm coming out of that painful place and I'm beginning to write.

My sense of that is I'm beginning to re-invert that which has been setting upside down for a while. I believe that is the process of recovery. To make this a little more direct, I'll give you an example from Jungian psychology.

Jung's measurement will show that somebody is an introverted thinker. My belief and contention is that the introverted thinker is the false self the child had to acquire in order to survive. Then he engages in the grief process, the discharging process, the acquisition of more soul, the more thorough recovery process, however you want to call it. He may turn and begin to focus back around and, lo and behold, after some many years, you find this person to be an extroverted feeler. And my contention is that he was an extroverted feeler as a child, but he could not survive that way.

David: So this is the true self emerging through the process, as opposed to the false self staying out in front and being supported by a whole set of false support mechanisms.

John: My sense is that the recovery movement and the men's movement are leading people back to the true self. Once the true self is activated, once the soul in the body has been activated, the ultimate result has to be: "I'll stop putting my shit on you." "I'll stop raping the land." "I'll stop projecting this repressed anger that I have for being an introverted thinker at my mother who made me that way to survive and become this." And then, "I can feel more deeply and I can feel the pain, because I felt the stuff about my mother and I can let go."

That's why in the Eastern traditions and in the fairy-tale traditions you find this wise old baby, like Lao-tzu. Lao-tzu means many different things, but one of the things he was nicknamed was "the wise old baby." He was the introverted feeler. Confucius was the extroverted thinker. Well, in many ways those are two archetypes for the same person, I believe. Through our evolution we go back.

An old man will be acting more like a wise old baby, a wise old child, than some wise old man. He'll say things that are so wise. Kind of the same things that two- or three-year-olds will say. He's made the full circle back to where he was before society, culture, mother and father started chipping away to make him into something he wasn't. His true self begins to return. And so at 65 years old he's wearing a baggy old set of doubleknit pants, and he doesn't give a shit who likes them or what's in style, just like a two-year-old doesn't care. What matters is what's comfortable, what feels good, what feels right because he's operating in many ways from a truer self. Whereas we're still going to the fashion halls to clothe the false self.

David: That answers a lot of my next question, which is what would be a list of needs, wants and characteristics that are possible for the adult male in the 1990s? And how is that list different from a parallel list that you might construct for the male in 1980, 1970, 1960, 1950 or whenever.

John: You know, the thing that comes out first and foremost is what started off this whole interview, and that's work. The 1990s male is going to want more time. He's going to demand more time. The healthier people become, male or female, they're going to demand more time to be with themselves, to be with their family, to be with the people they love, to be with nature. They're going to demand it, and I believe that they're going to demand more and more as they recover and as the settings they do work in become more and more functional and their bosses and supervisors become more and more functional.

David: Sure, because a recovering man (or woman) is not going to want to work in a sick organization. He's going to confront that illness quickly and say, "Hey, this is a kind of behavior I do not want to indulge in. If you want my skills in this job, then we need to straighten up this organization."

John: So I see the '90s also as being more the decade of the entrepreneur, the man working out of his house, that kind of thing, setting up small interconnected co-ops and then computer linkages because he is not going to be able to educate and recover the society as fast as he's recovering. But time is going to be the thing, I think.

NOTES

1. Robert Bly's books, pamphlets and tapes may be ordered from Ally Press Center, 524 Orleans St., St. Paul, MN 55107. Additional tapes may be ordered from New Dimensions Radio, P.O. Box 410510, San Francisco, CA 94141.

2. John Lee, **Flying Boy,** Health Communications, Inc., Deerfield Beach, FL, 1989.

   John Lee, **Flying Boy II: I Don't Want To Be Alone,** Health Communications, Inc., Deerfield Beach, FL, 1990.

   John Lee, **Recovery, Plain and Simple,** Health Communications, Inc., Deerfield Beach, FL, 1990.

   Information about John's tape series, his PEER (Primary, Emotional, Energy, Recovery) Training workshops and his other lectures and workshops can be obtained from the Austin Men's Center, 1611 W. 6th Street, Austin, TX 78703. Information about **MAN!** magazine can be obtained from the same address.

3. Robert Moore, a Jungian psychologist, may be heard on tapes from the C.G. Jung Institute of Chicago, 550 Callan Ave., Evanston, IL 60202.

4. Keith Thompson's 1982 interview with Robert Bly can be found in **Challenge of the Heart: Love, Sex & Intimacy In Transition,** ed. John Welwood, Shambhala Press, Boston, 1985.

5. Wilhelm Reich, **Bio-Electrical Investigation of Sexuality and Anxiety,** tr. Marion Faber, S.F.&G., New York, 1982.

6. Ken Dychtwald, **Body/Mind,** J.P. Tarcher, Los Angeles, 1986.

7. Martin Buber, **I & Thou,** tr. Walter Kaufman, MacMillan, New York, 1978.

8. Sierra Tucson, a treatment facility in Tucson, Arizona, that works with addictions and co-dependency.

9. Abraham H. Maslow, **Motivation and Personality,** Harper & Row, New York, 1970.

10. Thich Nhat Hanh, **The Practice of Mindfulness in Psychotherapy,** Sounds True Recordings, Boulder, CO, 1990.

KEN RICHARDSON

KEN RICHARDSON

Ken was co-chairman of the first conference dedicated to "Men, Relationships, and Co-dependency" held in 1990 in Phoenix. The next year he continued his leadership as co-chairman of "Tough Guys/Wounded Hearts," the successor to the preceding year's men's conference. Those conferences broke ground for all who attended by announcing that men's recovery engaged a different process than women's. Indeed, both conferences announced that men's process existed as an independent phenomenon. In 1990, 400 men and 75 women traveled to Phoenix from all over the country to share and learn from one another. In 1991 the conference was limited to 400 men.

At the same time that Ken works with men's issues, he is also involved, with his wife Mary, in relationship recovery work. He is currently Co-director of Phoenix Consulting and Counseling Associates, where he and Mary work with co-dependence, addictions, eating disorders, relationship problems and other dysfunctions. Ken also co-facilitates (with Curly Monroe) intensive men's wilderness gatherings. Earlier in his career at The Meadows[1] he was known as "The Velvet Hammer."

He was the Assistant Executive Director of The Meadows where he worked with the Director, Pat Mellody. There, he supervised a clinical staff of 17 family and primary counselors in treating a wide range of addictive behaviors. That work was an intensive summation of eight years of earlier experience in training clinicians and working as a therapist.

Ken has worked in the area of men's issues, addictive and compulsive behaviors, and family systems for over 15 years. He is a consultant, lecturer, therapist, and author who facilitates educational and experiential seminars around the United States and England. He has designed, developed and directed clinical treatment for various men's addiction treatment programs in Phoenix and San Francisco.

Ken and Mary founded and presently administer the Orion Foundation, which they established to meet the needs of Native Americans who suffer from alcoholism, drug addiction and related concerns. Their current project is the Hutoomkhum Support Program on the Hopi Reservation. Ken, Mary and their committee have developed an outpatient alcoholism and drug treatment program that is to be implemented on the three Hopi mesas.

The gentle and loving quality of Ken's presence attests to the depth of his recovery from co-dependence, alcoholism, drug addiction and sexual addiction. I met with Ken in his office in Phoenix in August of 1990. Our meeting had the quality of two old friends (or old souls) getting together after a long absence. Ken emphasized the spiritual nature of our journeys through recovery more clearly than anyone else I have spoken with.

INTERVIEW WITH
KEN RICHARDSON

August 1, 1990 • Phoenix, Arizona

David Lenfest: I'm curious to know how you relate to the notion of work addiction and how you define it; how you think it fits in the construct of your own life.

Ken Richardson: Well, I think it varies for many of us. Just as the driven needs behind alcoholism have nothing to do with alcohol, the driven needs behind compulsively working — busy-ness and not creating balance in my life — have little to do with working or being busy. Over the last three years, that's what I found myself doing. I'm not one to thrive on work. I love to be productive, to find new challenges and to be creative with those and to explore new avenues, but work for the sake of working doesn't interest me.

This morning I was in a 12-Step meeting, and all of a sudden I heard the word "accommodating." My co-dependent need to accommodate people's needs is part of what has driven my work addiction. I have accommodated many other people at the exclusion of meeting my own needs. It became clear that some of my accommodation of other people's needs has been out of fear of confrontation. Rather than do that, I'll accommodate what's going on and allow that to continue to happen. Then I'll carry my own feelings about it. Not saying no. I grew up with an over-heightened sense of responsibility. Six years in military school does that. The only time I can enjoy the goodies of life is if I have done all the work first.

David: Feed the troops first, and then you eat.

Ken: Right. Three weeks ago as a direct result of those misplaced priorities, I ended up cutting the end of my finger. It's just now healing, but I took off a pretty significant portion of it.

In June Mary and I took the first true vacation we had taken in three years. We spent two weeks in Hawaii. It took seven days to detox, and on the seventh day we had a major argument. All these feelings started coming up. It felt like when we had first moved into co-dependency recovery. All of a sudden it was really clear to both of us what had happened — that we weren't obsessively working and doing all the time, going at high speed and running here and running there. All the feelings that hadn't been dealt with were starting to come up. So we had a day's worth of feelings and then settled down.

Looking back to Phoenix from Hawaii was like looking into someone else's backyard and seeing all the issues that were there. It was a real shock. I had not recognized just how fast I had been going; how much I had missed myself; how much I had not been there for me but for everybody else; how many times I said yes when I should have said no.

David: Are all these things a consequence of your work addiction, are they a consequence of your accommodation or are the two so close that you can't distinguish between them?

Ken: The busy-ness is a consequence of my over-accommodations and not saying no, or my over-heightened sense of responsibility. Mary and I made a decision and took some time during that vacation to plot out what we wanted and what we didn't want. We plotted out a certain amount of time every week to be by ourselves, alone time with friends, time to play and to have fun, and time to work. We made major changes in our schedule for the next year as a result. We agreed to a certain number of commitments and so on. The first Saturday of our new schedule we were going to spend the whole day playing. We were going to go out to dinner, play pinball, go to a movie, just go play, whatever that meant.

To show you the difference in approach I'll tell you more about my finger and how it got cut. Before we left, we were sitting there having coffee in the morning, and I looked out in the backyard and said, "God, the yard's really a mess." (Laughter.) An old child-like sense of responsibility came up. I got this little tiny knot in my gut and I said, "Well, there's a couple of things we probably need to do before we go play." Mary was saying, "Yeah, I guess you're right."

None of it had to be done, but in my mind it had to be done before I had permission and had done "good enough" to be able to go play and just enjoy myself. So there I am trimming a bush at high speed with a little set of hand clippers, and I'm holding a bush and I just cut the end of my finger off. I was trying to get it done so we could go play. I was still trying to meet the roles and the rules dictated to me, especially in military school. Obviously I met a painful reality. It was another example of what I needed to do to start making some changes in my life again.

David: It's interesting the way the universe comes around and reminds us to pay attention.

Ken: Oh, yeah. (Laughs.) I know the feeling. I was on the phone telling a friend, who's a little odd, about what happened and he said, out of nowhere, "What did it sound like?" And I said, "I don't know, but I keep hearing the sound of scissors slowly cutting cloth." So it's like I hear that sound in my head, and it's a reminder, "Slow down, slow down."

We've been going at such a high pace for three years that to not do it has been difficult. I immediately go into, "What do I have to do? I've got something I have to do. I've got to take care of this. I've got to take care of that." It's more of my childhood that I'm becoming free from.

David: One of the things I was struck by at the conference that you co-chaired[2] in Phoenix was Shepherd Bliss' identification of men as "work objects" and how we're socialized to see ourselves as work objects.

That phrase alone has caused me to examine my whole working career, which I take back to age 13 when I started boarding school. I'm saying to myself, "If I'm not a work object and I don't produce all this stuff, then who am I? How do I value myself? If I can't value myself in that set-up, then I have to begin to see myself very differently."

Ken: I agree. I think being a "work object" is one of many roles that men have to take a look at. If we take the roles away, especially too quickly, we're left without an identity.

Our identity, especially where co-dependency is concerned, is based on the roles and the characteristics of birth order that are assigned to us in childhood. And we have lived out those roles and patterns over and over and over again as adults. The rules of dysfunctional families keep us locked into those roles.

David: I see, first child, second child and so on.

Ken: And hero, scapegoat, etc. Take those roles away — who's left? It was interesting. I had a good friend, a therapist, ask me one time, "Take your wife, your children, your job, the right clothes, the right car, whatever that is, the right house, the work environment, your friends, radio, television, newspapers, magazines, movies and artwork out of your life . . ." My eyes were closed. Then he said, "Now envision this." I said I did, and he asked, "Who's left?" I answered, "No one." And he said, "Hear who you call yourself?"

David: I hear that.

Ken: It brought up tremendous pain, and it was a graphic way to learn the fact that my identity was based upon things and roles. Take being the scapegoat out of your life. Take being the hero out of your life. Take being the worker and the provider, take the socialized norms out of your life. Who's left?

What recovery from co-dependency demands is that we go back and re-raise the child within, the male child or the female child. We must give them choices to be in one of those roles, whether it's appropriate or not to be in that role. Recovery is about choice. There are times when I choose to be in a hero role. I don't choose to be in a scapegoat role too much any more. But I have different guidelines for those roles today. So if I'm going to be a worker in this world, it's important to me to be a worker because I choose to do so, and I'm doing it for me first. I'm doing it from a balanced perspective, and I have choices.

Sometimes I don't. Circumstances dictate that I must do more than I want to do. I actually do that by choice, too, rather than "having to live up to" to be accepted by the world and fit in and be a part of.

David: I'm struck by your definition of our social roles in terms of wife, job, home, kids and that sort of stuff. What that parable immediately triggered in me was a figure in a desert landscape somewhere. It's always male. It's always he. And he's out there trying to survive in that landscape.

Ken: What comes to mind is the child. The descriptions I usually use to describe my adult life are those of the adult, the facade that I have created to be acceptable as an adult in the world. At that time, who really was left was a pain-filled, lonely, sad, shame-filled, hurt, scared, even terrified little boy who had learned over the years to not trust a soul. He had learned to stay hidden because it was too painful to stay out there and get shot at all the time or be abandoned, neglected or abused.

Today he's very much alive and thriving and growing and changing, which is, I think, part of any of our spiritual walks. We come to that part of knowing ourselves in one way or another.

David: Does that boy-child grow up? Do you have the sense that he's moving toward maturity, or does he stay in some age range that remains childlike?

Ken: I don't know. I haven't been far enough down the path to tell you from my own experience whether he does or not. His name is Tim, by the way. Tim was a childhood name given to me by my family to distinguish me from my father because I was "junior." So one of my roles was to be my father's junior. He was an abusive, violent drunk who died from alcoholism. At 28 I was dying from alcoholism and was an abusive, violent drunk.

I hated Tim until I moved into recovery from co-dependency and recognized that I didn't have to hate him for who he was. My Higher Power doesn't create junk. People taught me to believe I was junk or less than.

What I do believe has happened with Tim over the years is that I've been trying to develop a healthier child ego state, as opposed to a parent ego state or an adult ego state. We tend to be trapped between the child and the adult. But there's a parent on board that needs to be developed as well. Tim's become healthier, less fearful, so the feeling realities which the child part of my nature carries are not as extreme or as intense any more.

Today that natural child comes out more easily. It's not as difficult for me to go play with Mary. We go into supermarkets and we kind of get each other once in a while. I'll say things like, "Abortion, what do you mean you're going to have an abortion?" And watch the whole supermarket look and stare.

David: "And when did you stop beating your wife?" (Laughter.)

Ken: Exactly. Today Tim can laugh at that, delight in it, have a wonderful time with it, but six years ago — eight years into recovery from alcoholism — if I'd heard that, I would have gone into massive shame. I probably would have raged and told Mary to never, ever do that to me again. I would have said that because of the intensity of the feelings that the child part of me carried. I think the intensity of feelings dissipates, and the child comes more alive.

David: There's more play.

Ken: And more spirit. I believe it's the child part of our nature that carries the spirit of who we are.

David: One of my favorite books is Norman O. Brown's *Life Against Death*.³ In that book he corrects Freud's pessimistic conclusions. He contends that if Freud had followed his own logic correctly and observed correctly, he would have seen that "play is the highest form of human activity." For many years it has cheered me to think about how that idea might be the case.

Ken: I believe it. I think it's true, and it's one of the most healing experiences we can have.

David: It's funny, your sharing about the supermarket. I'm remembering back to one of the rare times that I

played with my older children. We were in a supermarket
in this sort of upscale section of Chicago that I was living
in, and it was a Friday night or something. I was a weekend parent, and we were going around in the supermarket
getting groceries for the weekend. Just for the hell of it,
I jumped in the cart and let the kids push me. (*Ken:* Oh,
how wonderful!) We just changed the roles, and the check-
out people and all the rest of the shoppers were totally
flipped. They couldn't quite put this together. (Laughter.)
This was 1970, '71.

Ken: Oh, oh, you do not act that way!

David: I'm sure I could hear them muttering, "That man
must be drunk." I might have been.

Ken: The child, Tim, came alive when I was drunk because the alcohol lowered my inhibitions and barriers.
The angry, bitter child that I was, the resentful, rebellious
child came out. I was either one or the other. You know,
"Mr. Charm" or "Mr. Enraged, Violent Man."
We're looking for the spiritual experience of joy and
delight in our life. Drugs bring that about. Alcohol brings
it about. But they all have their own down side as well.

David: Switching subjects slightly, Robert Bly talks a lot
about the importance of the Wildman or the Trickster or
the Coyote figure in men's lives, in changing men, in getting people across barriers between different stages in
their lives. Are you aware of having a Coyote figure or a
Trickster figure in your life? I know in your tape you
mention a teacher who taught you about sex and who
was sort of a father figure toward you.

Ken: Well, he was a therapist. I was in school at the
Devereaux Foundation in Victoria, and he was the only
therapist who didn't look over his glasses at me while he
was going "un-hunh" about the tests I had done. He ex-
plained them to me thoroughly and talked with me about

the variables involved. He actually put aside much of the "I'm the therapist, you're a kid who's here to see me because you have problems" role and developed a friendship with me.

In the process, he parented me by teaching me about who I was and about self-esteem and about sexuality. Of course, I thought I knew it all until he asked me to tell him what I knew, and I told him what I knew in about three and a half minutes. (Laughs.) He said, "No," and we spent a long time talking about sexuality, but he did it in a very non-shaming way.

Through that relationship, it was the first time I had ever felt like I fit in a school. All of a sudden I had all sorts of girl friends, I was very popular. And within a six month's span, I was invited to do everything with everybody. People wanted to be around me, and I didn't know how to handle it. I just sat back and went, "Wow, this is neat." Then they said, "You're well. Go home."

So they sent me back home, but nothing had changed in the family environment. Within three months I was back into the same roles, the same rules, the same characteristics of birth order, the same acting-out processes I had left about eight years earlier. That has convinced me that it's a family illness. It's not just related to one individual being a problem in a family. It's dictated and directed by dysfunction in the family system.

To go back to your question about coyote, Mary and I work with the Hopi tribe[4] in developing alcohol and drug abuse services. To them, coyote has a wholly different meaning than being a trickster in a positive sense. To the Navajos, coyote is actually evil. It depends on the tribe you're working with. There's a book called *The Medicine Cards*[5] written by Sams and Carson. It's a series of cards that have one animal represented on each card, and the book draws upon many of the various tribes' interpretations of each animal.

It's almost like a daily meditation. You just spread the cards out, pick a card and read the information on that particular card. Periodically I get the trickster, which is coyote, and the message is often that someone is stalking me and I'd better be careful. That someone is probably me, and I'm liable to trip myself up pretty quickly if I don't pay attention to what I'm doing. (Laughter.)

David: Or cut your finger with the hedge clippers?

Ken: Exactly. I did get the card at that time, by the way, right afterward. It's amazing how accurate the information has been about what's going on in my daily life.

I believe that there's a trickster side to our nature. Because we are cunning, baffling, powerful people, we have to have someone a little more cunning, baffling and powerful — or a trickster — to help us learn, to grow, to see. We can interpret whether or not that's evil, positive or negative. But I need to be tricked because I'm an analyzer who will try to control everything. My best efforts usually fail when I do.

David: So the Trickster is a device to defeat control?

Ken: For me, yes. It forces me, once again, to surrender and to do the Third Step[6].

David: For the Navajo and the Hopi, he's an evil figure. Tony Hillerman's most recent novel, *Coyote Waits*[7], has to do with an Anglo trickster figure.

Ken: I'm just reading that book, and I love his work. It's a fascinating way to learn about the Navajo nation and their spiritual beliefs.

David: One of the questions I'm trying to ask everybody is whether they're aware of having had a male initiation. You mentioned going to a military school for a number of years. Would you see that as your male initiation? Or would you point to other sets of experiences?

Ken: I think that in our society today we have very little formal male initiation, and that we tend to go through small initiations all along the way. The norm tends to do that. Being raised by two older sisters and my mother, I had no male in my life until I went to military school. I didn't experience those milestones that I needed to experience early in my life. I tend to agree that fathers are less likely to have the ability to initiate their sons than grandfathers.

David: Or their uncles?

Ken: Or their uncles. It's as though all the missing initiations and milestones that I needed to experience were crammed in a shocking way into military school. I was in a predominantly maternal environment for the first eight years of my life and then crammed into a militaristic, paternal environment. It was like going from one extreme to the other. It was a tremendous emotional shock. It was difficult for me to adjust, and I rebelled most of the six years I was in military school.

And, yes, a number of initiations took place, I think, through my life in military school in various ways, including some abusive initiations. I was sexually and physically abused in military school, also emotionally, spiritually and intellectually abused. That's part of the nature of the military beast anyway. These were unethical. I was physically beaten and sexually abused by a staff member and verbally abused and shamed. When I tried to tell my family what was going on, they'd say, "Oh you know that's just good for you. You know you got a lot out of military school. Sure did." (Laughter.)

I think that initiation, a true initiation, came for me through my relationship with Dr. Leighting, who was the psychologist who befriended me at the Devereaux Foundation. He really helped me make the transition from being a boy to a man. He was, I still recall, the only person who was really there for me, the only male who was genuinely interested in me. It was a loss when I had to come home.

David: I can hear that. What do you think about these initiatory ceremonies that groups like the Austin Men's Center and the Minneapolis Men's Center and people like John Lee and Marvin Allen and Shepherd Bliss are conducting? How do you feel about those?

Ken: I think they're vital and necessary. Our society has become lost in technology and compulsive behavior and has gone to extremes in those areas. It's time that we come back and remember our true nature and, hopefully, balance those extremes. I think they fulfill a tremendous need in men; number one, to bond with men, and also to experience other men in a way they may never have experienced men before.

David: I felt a phenomenal amount of trust in a group of 100 men when I did a weekend with them. It was a community of shared trust, and that was just extraordinary because the other groups of men I've been in — boarding school, college, the Army — have all been highly competitive. And the ultimate part of those institutional processes was that you were being honed to be some kind of hunter/killer.

Ken: Sure, survive the real world.

David: Basically, you were like a young brave getting trained to go out there and do battle with your brothers. Now people like John and Marvin and Shepherd are turning that around and saying "No, you can trust your brothers. We can be a community of support for each other."

Ken: I think we are now learning how. But, among other things, they serve as an example that it's possible, that we can work together instead of being on opposite sides of the fence. We've been doing men's circles here, out in cooler country, 50 or 60 men at a time to address these issues. Trust happens immediately. It's an amazing thing to watch. I'm in awe of it, somewhat fearful of it, again because of my history. It's become easier for me to become a part of that.

The feedback we've received from men is that it was a whole new awareness to experience male energy. It wasn't what we thought it was going to be. I believe male energy is a very rich and gentle energy, and that the harshness of traditional male energy has much to do with men's needs not being met.

Harshness is bred into us by society, and again by family systems, and again by the rules and roles taught to us and the suppression of intense feelings. When feelings become overwhelming, they have to come out in certain ways. And if society only gives us limited ways to allow that to happen, then a man's identity surfaces in only those ways.

David: I know that despite all the work I had done before the conference in Phoenix, I came away from it with a kind of simple-minded observation that: (a) it was okay to be a man, (b) it was okay to be a man and have my feelings and (c) I didn't have to perform a heroic act in order to experience those feelings or share them. It was like a revelation. I've really been a changed man since then.

Ken: Wonderful!

David: Maybe I've been leading up to it all these years, but I also feel the loss, too. I say to myself, "Well, my God, why couldn't I have known that before?" in the way that I came to know it there.

Ken: I think great truths are simple. It sounds like it was an incredible revelation.

David: It was!

Ken: To think it here (touches his head), but then to experience it and feel it here (touches his heart).

David: All my workaholism was directly related to my inability to give myself permission to express my feelings.

If I worked hard enough and achieved a big enough prize, you know, brought home a big enough buffalo, then I was allowed to have feelings for 30 seconds.

Ken: Right. Feelings of joy and excitement. God forbid that you ever got pissed off.

I see the men's movement generating major changes for men over the next few years. Many of the women of this country took the courage to do this for themselves a long time ago. And they had to generate some pretty powerful and aggressive energy to make it real, to make themselves known as women and to develop an identity, sometimes almost to an extreme. My hope is that the men's movement does not have to move to that extreme — that very early on we can see that we are all both masculine and feminine energy, and we must learn to balance that. That's when true healing happens and it is happening now.

David: One of the problems I see standing in the way of that goal is that there are a lot of women, professional women, business women, who have taken up the traditional men's path, even to the point of having heart attacks. They're very aggressive and very hard-edged . . . Anyway, there are many women who have taken up a negative, aggressive male energy in the way they relate to other people. They are as difficult as, if not more difficult than, men in traditional corporate positions. I think a lot of alienation has occurred as a result, and that there are a lot of men who are very chary.

I think that in some environments, it's really difficult for men and women to become friends now because it's difficult to get over all the stuff that has come around. It's almost as if we're at the point of getting ourselves together, wherever we are in the men's movement. I've had years of hearing about women, and I'm up to my neck in that. I don't want to hear much about it any more for a while. (*Ken:* Right.)

For the moment, I want to put the focus on men. And then when it comes time for integration, it's time for integration.

Ken: I think we have to put the focus on men now. It's like a pendulum. We have to make the swing to the opposite side before we can come back and find a balance point. Women taking over traditional men's roles and vice versa shows us that it's no greener on the other side of the fence. The issues may be different, but the benefits are no greater on one side than they are on the other. It's a personal goal for me to strive for balanced energy. I went from feminine energy as a very early child up to about eight years old to extreme masculine energy, and then I continued up to where I almost died from my alcoholism at 28 — enraged, violent, abusive, living what we call that masculine energy out to an extreme. Struggling in recovery to find a balance in there is vital for me. It's where I feel the most healthy. That and leaving enough room to move back and forth and to rely on my masculine and feminine energies, depending on the need and circumstance.

David: Well, I certainly hear that as a goal. I'm not quite there yet.

Ken: I don't know if any of us are, but I think it's where we'll have to move if we're to heal this earth.

David: Absolutely, right. Well, in this context of doing my own work with addiction, reading around in the field and doing my homework, this question occurred to me. Do you think that for a man, a break with his mother is similar to a break with his addictions?

Ken: Interesting question. I'd have to really give that some thought. My first response is that I believe that parents, male or female, who foster unhealthy, inappropriate dependence out of co-dependent, alcoholic or drug-addicted dynamics in a family system will set up a situation where a male child will experience the same kind of trauma breaking from a mother that an addict may experience breaking from an addiction.

The degree to which mothers or fathers foster the child's dependence, and the degree to which that dependence is reinforced through other compulsive dependent behaviors in the family system, will dictate how severe the break is going to be. If there's enough dependence fostered, then, yes, the trauma will be severe, or co-dependent basically. And the addictive co-dependency will be as severe a trauma as an alcoholic breaking from drinking. Much of the responsibility for that lies with the parents.

I believe that "God has no grandchildren." I also believe that we all — young children, parents, grandparents, aunts, uncles, all — have a direct line and a direct relationship with a Higher Power. Parents often times sabotage that relationship. We don't get to our Higher Power through our parents.

David: I find your answer really interesting. I guess that when I framed the question, what I had been thinking about was that when we break through an addiction to alcohol or drugs or whatever, there's a learning process we go through. We learn something about ourselves. We grow and we become better spiritual persons than we were when we were hooked on something outside ourselves.

As men, when we break away from our mothers, whether we do that early or late, there's also a learning experience that occurs. And if we follow the parallel, we'd probably want to explore what kind of spiritual growth occurs as a consequence of breaking away from her.

Ken: Spiritual growth is a direct benefit of breaking away from mother or father. Until we break away, Mom and Dad are God. They have the power to affect our well-being at any given moment. And the only entity in my life that should have that kind of power is my Higher Power.

If I give that power away to you, or to my parents, or to whoever (*David:* Or to the bottle?) or to the bottle, or to the drug, or to the food, or to sex, that becomes my God. How many people do you hear in CoDA talk about the fact that they haven't really broken away from their parents yet? They are 30, 35, 40 years old and Dad is still running the show or Mom is still controlling them. She can call them on the phone, and terror strikes. And they will not tell her what they would tell any one of their friends if the friend talked to them that way. That's giving the power of God away to another person, to a parent.

David: I remember that I was truly struck when I heard Pia Mellody's[8] definition of love addiction — that love addiction occurs when we put another human being in the place of our Higher Power. So we put this other person that we're in relationship with in the place of that Higher Power.

It's your idea that God has no grandchildren. When you said that, I thought about the times I have been addicted to different relationships, and I know now that I tended to put the relationship in the place of HP.

Ken: In my first marriage I married my mother. In my second marriage I married exactly the opposite personality. The third was my mom again, and the fourth was exactly the opposite. The fourth would have gone down the tubes within nine months had it not been that both of us were willing to recognize we were not going to be each other's moms and dads, and that we were going to start developing our own relationship and boot them out of the house. (Laughter.)

David: The crowded bed.

Ken: That's when our marriage and relationship began to become fulfilling. When I broke with my mother at age 37, I could begin to have a true relationship with my wife. I never knew until that time that there was a little boy inside me who was still looking for mom to fill the empty parts of my being, to do what hadn't happened with my mom in my childhood. To fix the abandonment, to fix the losses, to nurture me, to do the things I needed my mom to do.

David: Right. That's very hard information to give yourself and to accept. There's a lot of sadness and loss that goes into accepting that.

Ken: The destroyed relationships and destroyed marriages and the children that didn't get what they needed out of those relationships and marriages were directly related to my inability to let go of my past. I mean, I wasn't even conscious that I needed to do that. That's, unfortunately, the delusion of dysfunctional family systems. We grow up thinking everything is wonderful. It's painful, and it's an illusion that takes a long time to grieve.

David: Well, certainly we're all talking about the same age range. We don't really come to maturity until our late 30s, probably mid-40s? (Laughter.) Maybe early 50s? Somewhere in there.

Ken: And yet there are younger and younger people who are beginning the maturation process through recovery every day. It's wonderful to see. I'm delighted that they'll be able to gain the benefits at a much earlier age and not have to go through the losses that many of us went through.

David: Well, I think that's one of the benefits of mentoring younger men. John Lee and his men's groups have been advocating that. That work comes from a combination of 12-Step recovery programs and the conscious men's movement. It's a place where the two absolutely come together.

Ken: I think they have to, somehow, or the principles that are found in co-dependency recovery come to people through other means. I think those same principles are universal; in a way they're universal law. There are many people in recovery who have never gone near a 12-Step program, but they have, in one way or another, found their way to learning those truths and those principles and applying them in their lives anyway.

David: We've covered a lot of ground. One question I raised with Pat Mellody is that many of us as men are brought up to believe that there is some loosely defined code of behavior out there, whether it's a Boy Scout code of honor or military or Marine code of behavior. Following that code, or a different unwritten code of behavior that goes with class and responsibility, is a male duty. What was your sense of a code that was either implicit or explicit, or both, when you were a kid, and how did you relate to that?

Ken: When I was young, there was an implicit code. It was what we now call the rules of dysfunctional families. Those rules were very seldom ever spoken. And they could be changed at any given moment, depending on the needs of the adults in the family system at a particular time. They were often confusing. Nonetheless, they're imprinted on children in family systems, male children as well as female children. Depending on the dynamics of the family system, I believe we grow up to find social groups and gatherings that believe in the same or similar unspoken, usually subconscious rules because they feel normal and familiar to us.

We attract to us mates who either reflect the same kinds of rules we know or complement them in the opposite extreme. And then we butt heads. "Your rules don't match mine, but we don't even know we have rules, and we don't know how to talk about them because we were never given permission. So we just butt heads all the time, not knowing it's the family system that is still driving us." Mine changed a lot. There were certain specific rules we abided by. "No one gets angry in my family." Women especially. Yet my job as scapegoat was to soak up all the anger in the family that nobody was dealing with and act it out. Then I had the finger pointed at me and they sent me away.

I went to military school and the rules changed. They were very, very rigid and extreme. After a few years, I started slowly but surely rebelling against the rules because they were too rigid and extreme. There are social norms that apply to men and women. We go to great lengths to rebel against them. Then we come to a point where we have to take a look at the rules and ask if they are the ones we want in our rule book. Usually, we redefine them. Recovery demands that we redefine the rules.

Recovery redefines the rules for what it means to be a man. Today, for example, in my own values or sets of rules that I try to live by, it's okay for a man to cry. A man needs to cry. And a man needs to be angry, but he has to use anger appropriately.

David: I think John Lee has been doing extraordinary work in that vein both in his book, *Flying Boy*, which has sold 60,000 copies and in his Wildman weekends. He talks a lot about crying and how that is a normal part of the process of what we used to call "gettin' your ya-yas out." Grieving is just another, healthier way to do it instead of getting drunk and beating somebody up in an alley. Now you go cry and beat up the pillow. You don't destroy yourself or some other person or some property.

Ken: Fear is another one. Men are taught not to be afraid. Children get up and they come running into the room because lightning and a storm has scared them. And the first thing Mom or Dad says is, "Don't be scared. Don't be afraid." My mother used to say, "Don't be scared. Here, eat this. Pop," and she'd pop a Twinkie into my mouth. She suffered from an eating disorder and weighed some 300 pounds. She used food to fix both her and our feelings.

The earliest message I remember about fear is, "Don't be afraid." Some social groups at school were called "Scaredy cats." Fear was seen as a very disgusting, negative thing. That child part of me was put aside that way.

And then I was driven by fear, but I didn't know it was there. So I responded to the world as an adult out of fear, especially the fear of being shamed one more time or found out or caught again. And then somebody came along and said, "Well, tell me about your fears." And I went, "What fears?" It was a surprising experience to do a fear list.

David: I don't think I've ever done a fear list. Could you describe what one is?

Ken: The way it was described to me was to make a list of all the words I used to describe fear — scared, uptight, terrified, a little anxious, all the television words we use to cover feelings. And then I made a list of everything and anything, no matter how small it was, that I thought I might be a little afraid of.

I wrote and I wrote. When I finished, I had three legal pages, which is 25 lines per page, or 75 items during that sitting that I was consciously aware of being afraid of. I couldn't believe how much fear had been driving my behavior on a daily basis. And right underneath the fear was the pain. The pain came up and the grieving began and the losses began — and the fear subsided.

For me, pain is the core feeling. That's where the true healing comes from. The gift in pain is healing. When our leg hurts, we go get healed. When our emotions hurt, we push them down. On top of the pain was the fear, predominantly the fear of shame. On top of that was the anger. I had to get through the anger to the fear, then to the pain. I found out I was as addicted to fear as I was to alcohol or anything else. Fear was my automatic response.

We're an extremely fear-based society. And shame-based. The fear of shame is greater for me than the shame itself. I'll go to great lengths to guard and protect and keep everything in order to control and manage and manipulate a situation so I won't have to feel any shame about doing it wrong, looking dumb, stupid, foolish, inadequate, not fulfilling the rules of manhood, not living up to, etc., etc., etc., so then I'm acceptable to the human race.

When somebody comes along and says, "Boy, you really screwed up. You're not acceptable here," the massive shame from my childhood comes up and I want to kill myself. Looking at the fear was a major step in owning my humanness. I'm a fearful human being at times. My work in recovery includes learning to become less and less fearful, allowing my Higher Power to do its job and allowing you to be you and me to be me and not live in fear of what you might think or say or do in response to me.

Co-dependency on a spiritual level is a conflict in gods.

David: That's wonderful. Yes, that's exactly right because if you're love-addicted, you have supplanted your Higher Power with a person whom you're love-addicted to. Or if you're addicted to alcohol, you've replaced your HP with a bottle. And so on, all down the line.

Ken: I will go to great lengths to play God in my relationship with you to make you okay. I'll do this, I'll do that, I'll fix this, I'll change that. I'll control this. I'll do whatever I've got to do to make you okay *because* you're my God. If you're okay with me, then I'm okay. So I'll play God to make it okay. If you've accepted me, then I'm all right. At the moment all that's going on, there's no room for a greater spiritual force to be active in my life. I block it out immediately because I've given my attention, focus and direction to you as the person who will make me okay. *Progressive co-dependency is about spiritual death.*

David: I think that concept is not very well understood at all. I don't think I've ever heard it expressed as clearly as you've just put it.

Ken: Thank you. I can say that whatever entity I give my power away to at any given moment will become my God. I don't know that I'll ever be in a position where I don't do that at times. We all do it as we progress in our recovery.

My understanding of a Higher Power and the force of that Higher Power can be more powerful in my life as I quit giving power away to people, places and things to get them to tell me that I'm a worthwhile human being. And if they're dissatisfied with me, then I must be junk.

David: We're back again to, "God don't make no junk."

Ken: It's a vicious cycle. (Laughter.) It's childhood, here and now and my future all wrapped up in one.

David: That's a wonderful way into the whole thing. It's curious that the concept of "the code" would have led us to this very complex answer. (Laughter.)

Ken: I substituted the word "rules" for "code."

David: Sure. I'm learning things, so much from talking to all of you in the process of doing this book. And of course I'm talking to all of you men who are out there on what Marshall McLuhan called "the leading edge of the trial balloon." (Laughter.)

But no, seriously, you guys are out there on the edge, so I'm really being stimulated a lot. I've had this curious kind of cross-fertilization in an idea from Pat Mellody, who raised a question from Maslow. He asked why we only recognize the needs that aren't being met? Quoting Maslow[10], he said, "A satisfied need is not a motivator." I thought that was an interesting idea. Later I was listening to a tape of the Vietnamese Buddhist monk, Thich Nhat Hanh, conducting a workshop with psychotherapists in Boulder, Colorado[11]. He was reminding everybody to take stock and be aware of the good things in their lives. He said, "Think of the times when you have a toothache, and think how that feels. And then think of how it feels when you don't have a toothache, and celebrate that non-toothache."

Do you think that's an important idea? There's so much we have in terms of material satisfaction, in terms of our conditions in life. Is this business of a satisfied need, or the "non-toothache," pointing to something we're not seeing?

Ken: I think it's unrealistic, almost fantasy, to think we can reach a point where we have finally "arrived." When I was younger, I used to think (because I heard it so many times), "Grow up! Just grow up." I often wondered, once I grow up, where do I go? Sideways? Laterally, what do I do? Where is up? Is there a standard of maturity? I don't think so. It's unrealistic to think that if I just do enough X, Y and Z, everything's going to be okay for the rest of my life.

Constant change and cycles will force me to continue to grow. Feelings are the best motivators in the world. As long as I don't feel about life, I'm apathetic and in a sense I'm dying rather than living life. Fear is a great motivator. If I'm afraid, usually I'll get off my butt and move. If I'm really excited about something, I'll get moving again. If I'm angry about something, I'll follow through and take care of myself and deal with that anger. If I hurt, I'll grieve and let go of the past so I can move forward.

I believe we can only move as far forward into the future as we are willing to let go of the past. It's the past that keeps me from moving forward. The farther I'm willing to journey into my past, into my history and relieve and release myself from its bondage, that's how far I can move forward into the future. (*David:* Wonderful!) I know that I've had periods of satisfaction when things feel balanced and I'm satisfied, but invariably I move out of those periods because my needs have been met.

My first thought when you began to ask the question about the "non-toothache" was that we're talking about two things. We're talking about satisfaction and gratitude. We are a very rich society. In some ways, we're spoiled rotten and compulsive and addicted and have instant gratification in just about every way you can think of. A recovering priest at the Franciscan Renewal Center here in Phoenix was doing a weekend retreat, and he said, "If you can maintain an attitude of gratitude for who you are at this moment, this day, and for what God's given you today, I can guarantee you that you won't drink today."

I lose sight of the richness and the fullness of my life periodically, especially when I start focusing on one thing or one person who's causing me a problem. My energy gets directed that way, and I lose perspective on the rest of my existence. I have to remember to go back and smell the roses and remember that I have a life outside of this particular issue, and balance it again. I think balance is the key.

David: Okay. that's very good. There are a lot of people who feel that competition is a good motivator and that it has many positive effects in getting people to do things. I often think of competition as being a function of fear and/ or shame. I wondered how you feel about competition?

Ken: An example occurred in the film that Shepherd showed at the men's conference. There's a mountain north of San Francisco — Mount Tamalpais, I think — and there was a race, the Mountain to Sea Run, I think.

David: I saw the end of it, the blind guy running the race being led by the sighted person.

Ken: Exactly. I saw some people fall, pretty severe falls, especially on the down side of the mountain because of the momentum and the loss of accuracy that speed produces. I watched people run around the people who had fallen — just charge right on around them. I thought how fascinating it would be to see someone stop to help someone back up. "I can get there, but maybe I can stop along the way and help my brother."

The film focused a great deal on the fact that one person was leading this blind man through the race at the same time that others were running around the people who had fallen. It was quite a contrast to see the two, the competitive nature of the other people in the race, and this one man leading this blind man, trying to help him in the spirit of cooperation to meet a goal of finishing the race. My preference between the two is for the spirit of cooperation. We're all moving somewhere, and that somewhere for me involves our purpose here, which is to love and be loved. That's the goal and that's about all we have to give to one another.

David: I respect that too. I think of that difference that we got into earlier talking about your experience in military school, my experience in a boy's school or experience in the Army, where all those environments are intensely competitive and you were very careful to figure out who your friends were and who your enemies were. Your survival in some sense depended on your awareness of whether people were friends or enemies.

I compare that ethic to the kind of bonding and support that I felt in the men's weekend I did with John Lee and Marvin Allen up in New Mexico, where there was support and recognition of everyone's humanity.

Ken: I believe competition has become one of the many ways that we deal with our sense of shame. If I can compete and do well enough, I'll be okay. Therefore, it makes the competition non-productive. Fixing shame doesn't ever fix it. With shame, we never compete enough. We have to compete again and again.

David: The image for me is that competition is like a ladder that you climb and the shame is like a water level that keeps rising behind you. And you're running up this damn ladder as hard as you can to keep from being drowned in this shame that's coming up behind you.

Ken: Great analogy.

David: When what you really have to do is dive off the ladder and dive down into the bottom of the tank and pull the plug.

Ken: Exactly. Like the joke of the guy hanging on the edge of the cliff who prays to God for help and God says, "Let go." And the guy says "Is there anyone else up there?" (Laughter.)

I like your analogy. We will have to turn around and dive in.

David: That's what co-dependency work is about, isn't it?

Ken: Exactly.

David: We've covered an immense amount of ground. There's just one other question that occurs to me. I owe Pat Mellody for this one also. If our lives mimic the lives and careers of animals, does that make them authentic? Can we think of animals in the wild as leading a successful life? If we think of a wolf up on the tundra in something like *Never Cry Wolf*[12] or if we think of an animal leading a successful life, do our lives and careers in any way mimic those of animals?

Ken: I'm sure they do because we are natural beings as well. We adapt to our environment and survive it the same as animals do. Otherwise we wouldn't be here. We'd be extinct. On a basic and instinctual level, I think we have a greater intellectual capacity.

I was just reading a novel called *The Sphere*[13] by the same author as *The Andromeda Strain*. a doctor?

David: Oh, Michael Crichton.

Ken: There's a passage in there where the psychologist finally enters the sphere, and this voice begins to talk to him. It's obvious by the end it's his higher self. The voice said that we think our nature is very different from the animals and what makes us unique and different from the animals is our ability to imagine. But one of things we do not do as human beings is take responsibility for our imaginings. We imagine good and evil, and we imagine right and wrong. Yet we take little control of our imagining. What we imagine we manifest, and it is the greatest part of our intellect and our intelligence. We perceive it as just a step in the process of intelligence.

I read that about six weeks ago, and it really jarred me. I look at what we are as a society, and what we have done is to manifest what we imagine. The more we live in fear and manifest imaginings based on fear, those become a reality. The more we live in love and manifest those imaginings, they will become our reality. What we imagine and believe about ourselves, we manifest and it comes to us. This, I think, really sets us apart from the animals.

Animals live on instinct, probably genetic memory and understanding. We do as well, but we don't take responsibility for the greater gifts we have.

David: In some sense a lot of the disease of our society — the garbage that we live in, the atomic waste we live in — is a product of the competitive spirit and the limits of the scientific imagination. Unfortunately, science is not really science. Science is only mechanics, and it has real limits. We don't let ourselves know that, because scientists took over power at about the time of Darwin and they haven't let go.

Ken: With the advent of the technological age, their power has increased massively.

David: Exponentially. They may be ending the world if we don't do something about it.

Ken: It will eventually put us back to our natural state, and we're going to get there one way or another.

David: Look at the 250,000-year lifespan of all this atomic waste. Where are we going to put it? We have a terrible problem because the stuff at Hanford, for example, is getting into the aquifers that feed the Columbia River. Well, do we take it out of Hanford and put it into

this salt-mine parking lot that we've created down in Carls-
bad, New Mexico, and declare that a "sacrifice zone," as
the Department of Energy has?

Ken: In a community just south of Phoenix, a company
from Atlanta is trying to create an area where many of
the states would bring their nuclear waste. It's sad to
watch what we're doing. Not only to the environment, but
to ourselves emotionally, spiritually, physically and socially.

And yet to the degree that's escalating, so is forward
thinking, recovery, change, growth and insight. If in a dysfunctional family system, you take one of five members
out of the family and into the recovery process, and then
they come back to the system, it leaves the next four people
to carry the disease. The one closest to the disease in the
family system will then start to act it out. That person
moves into recovery, and it leaves the next three people to
carry the disease. Then the next closest will start to act it
out. The acting-out escalates with each person.

We do that as a society. The more we understand the
concepts of recovery and apply them to ourselves, the
more we're going to see the opposite extremes happen
too, such as rape and murder and wars.

David: So there are people in recovery and there are
crack addicts.

Ken: Exactly. It's more obvious. We see it more clearly
today. People are talking about incest and rape and child
molestation and abuse as commonly as they talk about the
weather or what movie they're going to go to tonight.
Ten years ago, we wouldn't talk about those things at all.
The recovery movement and the men's movement also
escalate the negative side. They have to.

David: Right, and the same paradigm applies to society
as it does to an individual, that things have to get bad
enough for people to bottom out before they can think
about what they can do to cure themselves.

Ken: Hopefully, we will hit bottom before we destroy ourselves.

David: That's up to HP.

NOTES

1. The Meadows is an Addiction Recovery and Treatment Center located in Wickenburg, Arizona.

2. Conference on Men, Relationships and Co-dependency, April 1990, Phoenix, AZ, sponsored by U.S. Journal, Health Communications, Inc.

3. Norman O. Brown, **Life Against Death,** Wesleyan University Press, Hanover, NH, 1985.

4. Ken and Mary founded the Orion Foundation for work with chemical dependency among the Hopi. They also make available as part of Phoenix Consulting and Counseling a series of tapes on "Loving the Child Within" and the "Life Experience Workshop." Information about the Orion Foundation or Phoenix Consulting and Counseling can be obtained by writing to them at 321 W. Hatcher, Suite 108, Phoenix, AZ 85021.

5. Jamie, Sams, and David, Carson, **The Medicine Cards,** Bear & Co., Santa Fe, NM, 1988.

6. The third Step of Co-dependents Anonymous: "Made a decision to turn our will and our lives over to the care of God as we understood God." CoDA, Inc., Phoenix, AZ, 1989.

7. Tony Hillerman, **Coyote Waits,** Harper & Row, New York, 1990.

8. Pia Mellody (with Andrea Wells Miller), **Facing Co-dependence** and **Breaking Free,** Harper & Row, New York, 1989. For tapes, consult Mellody Enterprises, P.O. Box 1739, Wickenburg, Arizona, 85358.

9. John Lee, **The Flying Boy, Flying Boy II: I Don't Want to be Alone** and **Recovery, Plain and Simple,** Health Communications, Inc., Deerfield Beach, FL, 1990.

10. Abraham Maslow, **Motivation and Personality,** Harper and Row, New York, 1970.

11. Thich Nhat Hanh, **The Practice of Mindfulness in Psychotherapy,** Sounds True Recordings, Boulder, CO, 1990.

12. Farley Mowat, **Never Cry Wolf,** Bantam, New York, 1983.

13. Michael Crichton, **The Sphere.** Alfred Knopf, New York, 1987.

ROBERT J. ACKERMAN

ROBERT J. ACKERMAN, PH.D.

Bob Ackerman is a sociologist who has specialized in addiction recovery for adult children of alcoholics since earning his Ph.D. at Western Michigan University. He is chairman of the Mid-Atlantic Addiction Training Institute and a Fulbright Scholar, as well as being Professor of Sociology at Indiana University of Pennsylvania. His two most recent books are *Silent Sons* and *Perfect Daughters*. Those titles reflect his ever-present humor in the face of the difficulties of working in the field of addiction recovery.

His lecturing style is dynamic and funny, while his information is backed by solid statistical research. When his personal experience and empathy for his many clients are added, it is easy to see why Bob has appeared on the "Today Show," "Oprah Winfrey" and "Geraldo."

He shared some of his recent conclusions on gender-based differences and his views on men in recovery in an interview conducted during the Second Annual Conference on Co-dependency held in Scottsdale, Arizona.

His presentation was remarkable for its clarity around gender differentiation between sons and daughters of alcoholics[1]. Bob made a number of distinctions between men and women in recovery. His observations about men are most helpful in the context of this book. For example, Bob says "Silent Sons" often end a sharing of their disease with the statement, "That's the way I am" or "Take me or leave me."

He pointed to an "incredible rigidity" around the definition of male and female roles by both men and women who are adult children of alcoholics and to an intensification of feeling about these roles. "Silent Sons" are supposed to be more instrumental, effecting change in the world. They maintain a code of silence that enjoins them to "keep it to themselves" if they have feelings about events or issues.

Men often show anger when they feel hurt or other "negative" feelings. Anger becomes a mask for many other feelings. In men's socialization, it is permissible to be angry but not to show hurt. When Bob works with male clients, he often finds himself wanting to know what feelings lie behind his client's anger. Of the possible combinations of alcoholism in their parents' lives, "Silent Sons" found an alcoholic mother to be the worst, followed by both parents and then an alcoholic father.

Bob found men's isolation typified the situation that men had more friends, but less intimacy. These friends tended to be "friends of function" coming from work, golf, team sports and so on. The injunction to "Keep it to yourself" was observed in these "friends of function." This isolation occurs often because men have been socialized to feel inadequate to deal with their own emotions.

Men define themselves by their ability to tolerate pain and not show it — except, of course, for stress-related illnesses like heart attacks, strokes, ulcers, etc. They are barred from intimacy by an inability to receive emotional responses from others. In painting this lonely picture of the "Silent Sons" emotional landscape, Bob points to current issues that need work.

INTERVIEW WITH
ROBERT ACKERMAN

August 27, 1990 • Scottsdale, Arizona

David Lenfest: Tell me about your field.

Robert Ackerman: It is sociology, primarily sociological practice, which would be clinical issues. Most of my work is with children of alcoholics, adult children and family problems.

David: You're in the process of doing a book on male adult children. What is it that's distinctive in the life patterns or behaviors of male adult children that's markedly different from those of women?

Bob: I don't think the difference between men and women lies so much in the experience, what we could call the CoA (Children of Alcoholics) experience, or even what happened to you while you were growing up. I think that the vast difference is in how it's interpreted and then how it affects adult behavior.

There are a couple of real obvious differences. One is that rates of chemical dependency are much, much higher in sons of alcoholics than in daughters of alcoholics. That's the real obvious one.

David: The sons are much more likely to become alcoholics themselves?

Bob: Yeah, much, much more likely to become chemically dependent, particularly the sons of male alcoholics. To me the next obvious difference is the great distinction in how much males won't talk about it, compared to how much daughters of alcoholics will talk about it.

David: I would guess that's a problem in sharing their feelings?

Bob: To me, trying to interpret a lot of this, it's not just the sharing of feelings, I think it's a living out of the socialization process. I think it's a lack of awareness on the part of adult sons that there are alternatives available. And perhaps there is a stronger denial on the part of the adult son than the adult daughter. Not just that he was affected. You know, we can just deny that we were affected. But I think there's a stronger denial that there's anything negative in his life. In other words, "Yeah, that happened, but what's the relevancy of that to the fact that I have relationship problems? It's irrelevant."

David: "If I'm a strong adult male, I'm supposed to be able to handle my liquor?"

Bob: Suppose I say to you, "Well, weren't you raised in an alcoholic family? Wasn't there a lot of dysfunction? Wasn't your dad an alcoholic?" The answer would be, "So what?" That's where I start to see the differences. You can start to fine-tune it about differences between sons of alcoholic mothers, alcoholic fathers, both parents. Certainly a great distinction between adult daughters and sons is that daughters go for help many, many more times than the man does. The adult son is more likely to go for help if he has a behavioral conduct disorder problem.

David: Such as . . .

Bob: He gets in trouble with the law, such as DUI (driving under the influence), or he gets into some behaviors of violence. He does something that's noticeable that borders on conduct disorder, being deviant, getting in trouble. He's not likely to seek out help because he feels emotionally unfulfilled.

David: How do these tendencies on the part of adult sons relate to other addictions, say to work addiction?

Bob: In most of my research, overwhelmingly, men always mentioned their jobs. For example, in the research on 1409 women to put *Perfect Daughters*[2] together, you can go back and read every interview and you will never find the job mentioned one time! Ever! (Laughter.) Now you can go and look at all of my work on *Silent Sons*[3], and the job is always mentioned.

I think just because we have been more commonly identified by our occupations, that makes the word "workaholic" appear to be a male syndrome. When in fact there are just as many women who are workaholics, but their master status may not be their occupation. Whereas for men, we run into each other and say, "What do you do?"

David: Right.

Bob: Right. Well, wouldn't it be nice if we said, "About what?"

David: Or "Who are you?"

Bob: We don't get that. "What do you do" equates to "Tell me something meaningful that you do or something socially redeeming," which means "Tell me your job."

David: Or tell me something I can compete with? You're a professor at X and I'm a professor at Y and therefore . . .

Bob: Right. And from that comes this identity factor. One interesting thing is that there was a study done five or six years ago on corporate executives in America, and what do you think was the most common variable in their backgrounds? This study predominantly was on men. Most people thought we would be looking for, "Did they go to Wharton? Did they go to Harvard? What business school? Did they have an MBA? What training? Who was their mentor, etc.?" The most common variable in their background was that they all came from dysfunctional families.

David: And they shared that with you?

Bob: Isn't that interesting? It wasn't my study, but it was in the data. The interesting thing was that the disproportionate, overwhelming group of these men came from dysfunctional families. So on the one hand, there were a lot of traits and tendencies they had picked up which allowed them to be successful in these types of environments. The other thing that the study didn't mention, however, is that these men were in the highest risk occupations for alcoholism — upper-level management and corporate executives.

David: Right, because of all the entertaining and socializing that they have to do?

Bob: Just jobs or pressure or whatever it happened to be, it's all in there.

David: That's interesting. One of the things I've tuned into recently in the process of doing this book is the notion that, as men, we're socialized to be "work objects" parallel to the notion that women are socialized to be "sex objects." That is, we obtain our value through work.

Bob: I think that socialization pattern, though, is not just a work object pattern. I think that pattern is a given, and that it is such a given, it's not an assumption. The young boy in our culture is socialized not to question that when he becomes 18 or 20 or 22 or 24 he's going to engage in a particular occupation for the next 40 to 50 years.

Now that takes a lot of pretty interesting socialization, but it also takes away from the male thinking about it. See, it's a given that you're going to do this. So I think it's fascinating that on college campuses, the seniors are inundated with the question: "Well, what are you going to do now?" For young men there's this assumption. His answer is, unspoken, "I'm going to do what is expected of me."

How much latitude does he have? What is expected of him is that he will become gainfully employed. He doesn't initially have expectations of issues like, "Are you going to be a good father?" "Are you going to be a good spouse?" "Are you going to be a healthy human being?" "Are you going to be emotionally in touch with your life?" Those are not the kinds of things that we basically think about when we come out of those systems.

David: As you speak, I'm thinking of my own experience. I expected to be a parent, and a good one. I certainly was aware that I had grown up in a dysfunctional family, and I was aware that I was very relieved to go away to boarding school when I was 13 because it got me out of that family. And it got me into what was essentially a militaristic structure. But that was okay. It was better than the craziness I was living in.

And yet, somehow, I had the expectation that I was going to be a better parent than my parents had been. I was going to improve — one could hardly do worse.

Bob: I think one of the things that amazed me about many, many "Silent Sons" was an overly-developed sense of what our fathering responsibilities would be. I saw this much more in sons of alcoholics. I can remember sitting in on a conversation where there were three other sons of alcoholics and me. All of us had children, and all of us as fathers shared our sense of questioning. "Were we doing enough with our children? And for our children?" The consensus was that each one of us did about eight times more positive things with our kids than was ever done with us. And yet we were sitting there saying, "Is this enough?"

David: Is it good enough?

Bob: Is it good enough? Which means, "Are we good enough as fathers?" See? Or were we inappropriately projecting the contentment of our children as a reflection of our value as fathers?

David: Yeah, as a way to rate our performance as fathers. There we are again, rating ourselves in terms of what we do. I see that as part of the disease.

Bob: It's a performance standard out there.

David: Let me start a new line of questioning. Is a man's 20th century initiation grounded in the sorrow of his abandonment by his mother and father, his loss to and recovery from addictions and his re-emergence as a growing human being? Or do we see other kinds of initiations, or do we have multiple initiations?

Bob: I think I would reframe that and talk about male rites of passage. I don't see this thing being framed as a sense of loss or grief or separateness from our parents because we are raised with that expectation. We are also raised with the expectation that we will become independent. More interestingly, we are raised with the expectation that not only is it permissible, it's also desirable, acceptable and honorable to go beyond the accomplishments of your parents. Even your parents will take great pride in saying, "Look what our son, David, has done," or "Look how he lives." And they will take great pride in this.

I don't see this separation, therefore, as a great rite of passage, a great initiation. I see where the initiation comes from at some points, and I see this process getting longer.

I see a problem when the man finally says, "I am at an age and a position in my life where I'm the father" in kind of a generic sense. There's a classic scene in a movie called *Middle Age Crazy* when Bruce Dern is turning 40. His father was a powerful man while he was growing up. His father is aging now. Dern's character has children of his own. He's married. And now he finds himself in this incredible position of responsibility to both his aging parents and his kids, and he's in the middle.

So he runs out and buys a Porsche. He has an affair with a young girl. He does all these things to deny where he is. Finally it comes to the point that he says, "I don't want to be the father." He looks at his dad and he tries to figure out, "How did my father accept his role and do as well as he did? I don't want this."

And a very great scene happens later in the movie. His father dies and Dern goes to the funeral. He's sitting in the graveyard, and he's just kinda lost. His son, who's now 16 or 17, comes over to comfort him. He says, "You're the poppa now."

I see the rite of passage for American men to be when we no longer wrestle with becoming the father.

David: When we accept the role.

Bob: We accept it in all of health. Not as a dire necessity where we have no choice. We say, yes, this is my time, and I will do as well as I can.

I have always thought that my father was preparing me to take over when my time comes, and I will do that, hopefully, with our sons. I'm not saying a man will have to

be in charge of everything, but he's going to come to a
point in his life where he's going to be the father. That's
where I see the great rite of passage.

I see everything that happens before that, like getting
your driver's license, smoking and drinking, your first sexual experiences and all those other things as nothing more
than minor rites of passage.

There is one last comment that I want to make. In
China, and I think this is fascinating, no one has to listen
to you as an adult until your 40th birthday. (Laughter.) It's
kind of an interesting thing that up until then you're just
kinda getting ready.

David: As you say that, I'm thinking of a remark that I
heard a long time past to the effect that at 40 you've
earned the face that you wear.

That gets us around to ageism in a way, which is also
an important subject. I was truly moved when I went to
the Men, Relationships and Co-dependency[4] conference.
In the closing ceremony, they gathered all the men over 50
into a circle in the center, and they honored us for the fact
that we had survived that long through marriages, divorces, jobs, children, you know, whatever, you made it
this far. I was truly moved by that. I'd been trying to avoid
the fact that I'd crossed over the 50 boundary line.

This ceremony, in turn, encouraged all of us to start
mentoring the younger men. That's part of the men's movement stuff going around that I honor and I'm working
with. It just honored our experience as human beings.

Bob: I have had a feeling for a long time that the last
thing a man will do in his life of any meaning will be to be
a grandfather. That doesn't necessarily mean you have
grandchildren. It's the idea of what you're passing on. If
you can have that meaning — even though we are a society that is obsessed with youth, and even though we hate
our young people, which is an interesting dichotomy —
there is this idea more about who you are and who you're
capable of being and giving.

One reason I think men haven't given much, when we're criticized for it, is that I'm not too sure anyone has ever asked us.

David: When you say, "Men have not given much . . ." Given?

Bob: In other words, what men have given has been so taken for granted that when someone asks an older man, "What did you really give?" he might say, "For 43 years I got up every morning at 7:30 and I went into that steel mill, and I did this. And I put a roof over my kid's head, and you know." So what did you give?

On the other hand, when he's asked, "What did you give of yourself?" he says, "Well, nothing. They weren't interested."

David: When I interviewed Ken Richardson he told me a story that I've been sharing with other people, because it strikes me as one of the most significant bits that has emerged from these interviews. He said that a friend presented him with a parable: "Think of your job, think of your wife, think of your family, think of your home, think of your hobbies, think of your animals — and take them all away. What have you got left?" The answer was, "Nothing." The reply was, "Hear what you call yourself."

That to me is a central conundrum that we face as men. You're pointing to it, too.

Bob: That's an unfortunate thing. The pattern that you find in children of alcoholics and adult children of alcoholics is external validation, only.

David: You've done so much work with women. Do you think that a large number of men are raised by women in this culture to be naive?

Bob: Naive about what? (Laughter.) I have an answer for that, but you see what I mean?

David: I mean naive about the sense of self.

Bob: The first thing that comes to mind is that we're naive about women. That's usually what we're attacked about. "We have no idea what's going on here."
I don't see it as a conscious effort whatsoever. I would support that idea by saying that we are raised to be naive about our own feelings, our own emotions. I think we're naive about the fact that these feelings or emotions even affect us.

David: Or that they're valid?

Bob: Or that they're valid. And I think we're very naive when it comes to alternatives, other models, other ways that we can do these things. That's what would come to mind. But I would not support a notion that says women are responsible for the naivete in men. I don't believe that women create naive men, no.

David: That was the hook in the question. But lack of male validation does create . . .

Bob: Sure, but what may happen? Let me give you an example. Here's mother doing whatever, and we have this mothering going on. But if there's a father there, she may unknowingly do this behavior defensively, and the father unknowingly demonstrates it. So it's like a one-two punch out there, isn't it? If sons pick this up . . .
There's an interesting thing on kids and gender. It says that in our culture little boys know more about being a little girl than little girls know about being a little girl. That's because we've been bombarding little boys with rules that if they engage in emotional behavior, someone says, "Don't do that. Quit acting like a little girl." (Laughter.) "Don't be a sissy." But the interesting thing is that what the boy picks up is supposedly what girls do, and that what girls do is negative. Boys aren't supposed to do what girls do. But he's never told what boys do. There's the naivete.

"Big boys don't cry." You say this to your five-year-old. "Big boys don't cry." Well, then, what do they do?

David: They have no idea.

Bob: See, that's where the naivete may be.

David: Is there any kind of working model? It seems to me we've pretty well exhausted the models that have been around. Bly talks a lot about men's role as a hunter. He sort of idealizes that role, even if we're doing something else and the hunting is metaphorical or spiritual in some way. Then there's this whole business about male codes, whether they're Boy Scout or Marine or whatever. These again are all models, and I think they're all undergoing severe change at the moment. I wonder what you think of that concept?

Bob: I hope that there's change. And I think to a certain extent there is. One example is that fathers today, young fathers, are supposedly more involved with their children than at any time in history. There's a great majority of men who are spending more time and being emotionally involved than their fathers did.

On the other hand, I think the double standard is still alive and well in our country and we are still socializing men out there in this — you know, the strong silent type, the Germanic model, which then equates to "Keep it to yourself, hide your pain."

The interesting thing is, too, if we move it off the negative side, we get, "Don't show too much of your joy. Don't have bliss." So I see some changes, but I still see a fairly strong double standard. And I am seeing a lot of men breaking out of that. I would say certainly there are a lot more men breaking out of that model today than, say, there were in our father's generation.

David: Right, and that's what these Wildman's Weekends are about — an attempt to break out of that, isn't it? To experience our feelings, to be legitimate about that.

Bob: Right. I think there is a gentleness in males. But the interesting thing is that it is the strongest who display it.

David: How do you perceive that strength?

Bob: As an inner strength of knowing who you are and what you are about. It can even be equated with physical strength.

David: You mean like Rosy Grier[5] doing needlepoint?

Bob: Absolutely. Even to be trite, some of the largest, strongest, most muscular men "dare" to be gentle, because then they're called "gentle giants." (Laughter.)
What happens is that it is, in fact, the strongest of men who are gentle. What I mean by strength is a sense of well-being, health and feeling good about who you are. The healthiest people are emotionally androgynous. If men, unfortunately, are guilty, it's that we're relatively stoic and limited in our emotions.

David: Well, we're trained to suppress those emotions. We have to go through a whole retraining process.

Bob: Not totally. We are more trained to suppress them given certain conditions. That's what's interesting. Given other conditions, we don't have to suppress them.

David: It's part of the fight or flight response.

Bob: Yeah. So the question is, how do you make those transitions? I will not support statements that say men are not emotional. If you demonstrate to me the capacity to be emotional, then you are emotional. You have that capacity. What may be different is you may control them very strongly so you are rarely emotional or you are only emotional in certain situations. That doesn't mean that as a *homo sapiens* you do not have the capacity to be emotional.

David: I've been very interested to read and hear Terry Kellogg introduce the term "debriefing" when he talks about the validity of 12-Step meetings. He says the value of going to meetings is that it gives people a chance to share that pain, share those feelings and to debrief, to get rid of that stuff. That's the first time I've heard that, and it also has a male flavor to it simply because of its militaristic origins.

Bob: I think you're right. Isn't it interesting that the prisoner of war — the hostage for six years, five months and two days — is debriefed before the military will let him return to his family. The government steps in and debriefs him. Then look at a comparison between World War II and Vietnam veterans. The World War II veteran, on the average, took several months to get home. He spent time on ships with other men who had spent four years or three years or two years seeing the atrocities of war. While those ships were crossing the ocean, there was in fact debriefing occurring.

The Vietnam veteran, on the other hand, literally with only 15 hours on a commercial plane, was dumped at Traverse Air Force Base. And there was no one there to allow him to debrief. By contrast, people welcomed the World War II veterans home. This was different. Robert Bly talks a lot about men and their grief. Then he attacks this whole situation that America has never grieved over the Vietnam war. America has never been emotionally debriefed over this war. What do we do? We keep denying our emotions.

David: In your work with male adult children, you must see that process going on all the time.

Bob: You know I do. In some cases, I run into daughters who say to other daughters, "I'm an adult daughter of an alcoholic," and there's this, not negativity, but sort of like a neutral thing, or maybe just a slight bit of feeling guilty or feeling ashamed. With sons of alcoholics who reveal that to other sons, you get kind of a "Me, too; me too." I sense more of a relief.

David: Okay, so that's why the debriefing. "Well, gee, I'm not alone in this." When I first got into ACoA, my feeling was, "Boy, I'm not alone." My mother happened to have been the alcoholic, but I also ran into a lot of people who were recovering Irish Catholics, which seemed to be part of the same disease.

Bob: One of the things I've done with adult sons who are hesitant to talk is to ask, "Did you ever have to go and get your dad out of a bar?" "Oh my God, yeah." I call that "tavern duty." "You got tavern duty." You gotta go get your dad out of the bar. Well, there are lots and lots of sons who had alcoholic fathers who can relate to that right away.

What's happening, to use your phrase, is there's a debriefing, isn't there? There was this experience, this confrontational experience. You had to go get your dad out of a bar. I mean you were putting your life in your hands, one male to another, getting your father. I don't care if you were eight years old, 12 years old. Because they were all men in that bar, weren't they? And you were going in there to tell your dad, "Mom's outside with the car, waiting." This is Rome. This is "Kill the messenger."

I've used that many, many times as a way to get to a man who's not going to talk about it. It is that common experience that we can identify with, and then we can start to get to our emotions, can't we? We say "God, I hated doing that." Or, "I thought he was gonna kill me." Or, "I wanted to tell my mother, 'I don't want to do this,' but she was hurting." There's a way that emotions start to come out around that shared behavior.

I think this is where we as men are going to go. I think the whole adult children thing for sons is a way in which our emotions can start to come out around this shared behavior, whereas what I saw with the daughters was all this emotion and no realization of the commonality of the shared behavior.

David: That's interesting. In the male children, although it must be true for females too, it strikes me that there's an immediate loss of childhood. The mother appoints the child, the eight-year-old, the 12-year-old, to go drag Dad out of the bar. All of a sudden he's appointed to be an adult male.

Bob: This happens for daughters as well. But there's this reinforcement that says, "Act like a man, act like a man." We don't really hear, "Act like a woman." It's related to that thing about little boys knowing more about girls than they do about boys. So, when you say that, you're probably correct — do we have this thing on boys to grow up sooner?

However, there is a little contradiction among college students that's interesting. A study showed that for female college students of traditional age, the 18- to 22-year-old group, the college years are seen as a young adult period, a time to get ready to make that transition to being an adult. There is a lot of research today saying that same period for men is becoming nothing more than an extension of adolescence.

Isn't that interesting, you see? The key seems to be that until a man is out on his own making his own money, he doesn't have that transition. Most fathers hold that over the heads of their sons. "You're under my roof . . ." (*David:* . . . which means "You're playing by my rules.") "I am somehow economically involved, or your mother and I are economically involved." So you might as well act like a damn teenager.

There's some interesting stuff about college students, and I watch it in dating practices. I'm not so old that I'm that far removed from who's doing what on campus. It always amazes me to see that the woman is trying to become more refined and dignified and adult. Since these are the only guys around to date, most of the women are putting up with this childish behavior from the males; drinking, breaking furniture, partying, hard-charging, going out and fulfilling these very stereotypic roles.

David: That's interesting. I hadn't thought of that as a differentiation because I would have written it off to the classic distinction that women mature earlier. This idea has more substance to it.

Bob: The idea that women mature earlier has always been ascribed to the argument of physical maturation and engaging in behaviors that adults find socially acceptable. The male doesn't have the physical maturation as early, but he is also likely to engage in conduct disorders for a longer period of time. His behavior is more obvious, like hard-charging around in a car, or whatever.

David: Let's go to a new question. How about a list of needs, wants, characteristics that are possible for a man in the '90s, and how is that list different from previous decades?

Bob: I'm not sure I would see it as different from previous decades, even previous centuries. What could be different is our level of awareness of these needs. In other words, I think these needs have always existed, but we're coming closer to recognizing the needs and the legitimacy of those needs.

I think we're coming closer to men realizing there's got to be more to life than this. Men saying, "Whatever this life is that I have right now, this is not a rehearsal."

David: Or I'm not going to put myself on hold until I'm 40. I want to be involved.

Bob: What do I see as needs for men in the '90s? I definitely see that we need to provide more men's groups. I think we need to be able to provide a resurgence, as Robert Bly says, in mentors, and that's going to happen when men begin to feel good enough about themselves to share themselves. One of the reasons we may have gone through a period that lacked mentors is that men may not have been feeling good about themselves.

David: Bly has the contention that we lost our warrior status in Korea and in Vietnam, particularly, and that this condition contrasts strongly with the Japanese. They may have signed a treaty for total surrender at the end of World War II, but they have re-emerged as warriors for armies called Sony and Matsushita and Datsun and so on. And they're very successful warriors at what they do.

Bly says that we have lost that, somehow. The question he leaves hanging in the air is, "How do we get that back?" Do we get that back through this process of getting in touch with our feelings, owning our feelings, being who we are, or do we really get into tough martial arts training, or what?

Bob: I would counter that with a question that says, "Do we want that back?" Because I'm not sure the warrior mentality was the best way to be in the first place. So I would ask, "How do we find a more suitable replacement?" As a man, I would like to be identified with more than an adequate warrior. Because there are days that I say, "I'm tired of fighting."

That will be the challenge for the '90s.

David: There are days that I want to sit here and watch the leaves fall.

Bob: That's right, and not feel that I have to rake them. (Laughter.) God put those leaves in my yard, God can take them away. So how do we expand our roles beyond being a warrior? I'm not sure that we want that back.

It's just like this current Iraq thing. Are we supposed to jump up and down and say, "God, thank God, now there's something for men to do." (Laughter.) Is that the limit of our development? Is that what we're saying?

David: I think there's a lot in question there. I am enough of a veteran of the peace movement in the '60s that when they started the expansion in Iraq, all of a sudden the question came back to me, "Suppose they gave a war, and nobody came?"

Bob: Somehow that double standard is alive and well, because everybody is . . . See, everybody, until they realize that war means people get hurt and people die . . .

David: Until the body bags start to pile up . . .

Bob: Right.

David: Of course, it's a co-dependent kind of war, too. Tom Wicker pointed that out when he said that the oil primarily was going to western Europe and Japan, yet it was our troops over there defending it. We're the co-dependent, whatever gender we might be. We're picking up the bill.

Bob: Is the United States the man who unquestioningly goes to be a warrior?
Mark Twain's *War Prayer*[6], for which he is not known, talks about going to war. He talks about a thesis and antithesis that if you pray for victory, then you are praying that *their* sons will be blown apart and killed and that there will be widows and orphans in their country. If you pray to smash your foe, then you hope they are destroyed beyond all recognition. So, he wrote this thing called *The War Prayer,* which says that if this is what you pray for, then you realize you're going to get both sides.
He left very strict instructions that *The War Prayer* not be published until after his death. That was a part of Mark Twain that he couldn't share while being alive because that was a part that wasn't going to be accepted by people. Isn't that interesting?

David: Despite all the satirical and sarcastic things that he had to say . . .

Bob: Look who he wrote about — boys. He wrote about boys, didn't he?

NOTES

1. "Perfect Daughters and Silent Sons: The Three 'I's' in Recovery (Isolation, Inadequacy and Intimacy)," Robert J. Ackerman, Second Annual Conference on Co-dependency, Scottsdale, AZ, August 27, 1990.

2. Robert Ackerman, **Perfect Daughters,** Health Communications, Deerfield Beach, FL, 1990.

3. Robert Ackerman, **Silent Sons** (Work in progress).

4. Men, Relationships and Co-dependency, Phoenix, AZ, April, 1990, U.S. Journal, Health Communications, Inc.

5. Roosevelt Grier played fullback for the Detroit Lions. He performed on **"Sesame Street,"** and helped to produce a tape for children, **Free To Be You and Me,** Arista Records, 1972.

6. Mark Twain, **"The War Prayer"** in **Mark Twain and the Three Rs,** ed. Maxwell Geismar, Bobbs Merrill, Indianapolis, 1973.

TERRY KELLOGG

TERRY KELLOGG

Terry Kellogg is well-known for his expertise in family systems therapy. His work with sexual offenders, sexual abuse and addiction therapy has been influential. His pioneering work in the development of theory and treatment for co-dependency is not nearly so well recognized by the public as it is by professional "insiders."

In 1982 Terry founded the Compulsivity Clinic, which later became the Lifeworks Clinics. They are presently held in seven states, presenting a healing process for people with relationship or family problems as well as for people who grew up in alcoholic or other dysfunctional families.

Terry is also a faculty member of the Institute for Integral Development, the Listen to Learn Resources Group, and the U.S. Journal. He was featured on John Bradshaw's PBS series "On the Family," which was based in part on Terry's original work. He does over 100 lectures a year, and he has appeared with Phil Donahue, Geraldo Rivera and on other major TV programs.

Terry's most recent book is *Finding Balance: 12 Priorities for Interdependence and Joyful Living*, co-authored with Marvel Harrison. His 1990 book, *Broken Toys, Broken Dreams*, summarizes a great deal of his earlier work on the treatment of the wounded inner child. Throughout his work, Terry is remarkably clear in demonstrating the connections between the inner child and the addicted or co-dependent adult.

Terry's gift for sharing a sympathetic and warm approach to human problems was evident when he led the Second Annual National Conference on Co-Dependency[1]. In his address on "The Inner Child's Big Picture: Integrating Childhood and Adulthood Spirituality and Sexuality," he emphasized the predicament of the wounded inner children who grow up denied the opportunity to depend on their parents and, consequently, become unable to depend on themselves.

Indeed, Terry believes co-dependency is "an absence of a relationship with the self." Another striking perception of his work is his understanding of co-dependency as a "sibling" of PTSD (Post-Traumatic Stress Disorder). People suffering from co-dependency, like those who have survived wars and other major traumas, are subject to "flashing back" to earlier feeling states, particularly ones that were suppressed and not finished.

In Terry's view, fear and hatred of one's own vulnerability characterize both the co-dependent and the person suffering from PTSD. Ultimately, he sees an addict as a person who has closed the door on his or her own choices. These people — the co-dependent, the PTSD victim and the addict — live in a culture that hates fear and vulnerability. In his emphasis on interdependability, Terry is opening again, "the territory ahead."

When I interviewed Terry in Scottsdale at the Princess Hotel where the conference was being held, he was immediately recognizable as the man gliding along on bright green roller blades. Terry's sense of humor is always present to leaven the seriousness of the problems he confronts.

INTERVIEW WITH
TERRY KELLOGG

August 27, 1990 • Scottsdale, Arizona

David Lenfest: Would you care to comment on our roles as men these days?

Terry Kellogg: My impression is that we probably aren't going to do a great job of defining ourselves and our roles as men until we define more about our human experience and the integration process. I think there's a tendency in codependency to polarize. In that polarization process we go from rigidity to irresponsibility, over-responsible to irresponsible swings. We go from perfectionism to looseness and from being in control to being out of control.

David: In a way, I'm thinking of the women's movement when women, say 15, 20 years ago, began to gather and identify themselves as a

gender and began to identify issues for themselves. They
created ways they could feel good about themselves as
women and not as victims. That process empowered them
a lot, and I'm wondering if . . .

Terry: It did some, but I think it didn't empower them as
much as it could have because the result of the women's
movement has been some wonderful ideas that seem to
have been lost. What I'm trying to do is to retrieve some
of the ideas of the feminist movement by utilizing a style
and approach to therapy that I call interdependency, which
has more to do with the integration and the egalitarian
nature of what we do and who we are. That approach
points to sameness, not necessarily equality depending on
roles, and a respect and a learning from each other.

In the name of progress, men and women now get to
participate in each other's pathology. Men can take their
clothes off on stage and have women tuck money in their
G strings, and women are now dying of heart disease
from running and owning their own corporations.

I like the concept that when women wanted what men
had in the white male system, which was power, they
missed the fact that men's power is the source of their co-
dependency, which is the inverse of women's!

David: They also missed the fact that power has a price.

Terry: Yeah, but power is the illusion. Men's power is
their powerlessness. See, women's co-dependency is their
power through powerlessness. Men's co-dependency is
powerlessness through power.

David: Would you want to expand on that?

Terry: Okay. Women's co-dependency is rooted in being
taught powerless roles. That's why it was called "the
spouse disease." Co-dependency got seen as the victim
posture, a powerless posture. We missed the fact that in
polarization the victim and the offender are in the same

line and that they have the same issues. It involves a basic victimization, an absence of boundaries, an absence of identity, integrity and developmental formation that gets expressed in different ways.

Humans and human systems are so complex that you can't put things in a box and say, "Because this happens, that will follow." But you can generally say that when something goes awry, there will be a polarized result, or something extreme will happen in some area.

David: There will be a swing, the pendulum . . .

Terry: Right, some people go back and forth. What happens in our culture, then, is that women are taught powerless roles, and so they learn to exert a lot of power within those roles. Some have seen that as manipulation, but women learn to operate their power covertly.

Then a 12-Step program is written, but it's men who wrote it. And the First Step[2] is coming to accept that our lives are unmanageable, powerless. To a man walking into the program, "Man, that feels wonderful. Wow! My God. Other people feel powerless."

But a woman walking into the program says, "Hey, my life is unmanageable, I'm out of control. So what's new? No great shakes." (Laughter.) Women working the First Step have to go through a two-stage process, really. They have to look at the power beneath the powerlessness, and then the powerlessness beneath that.

Men are taught the power roles, our co-dependent posture. We are the economic symbols, the power objects, the expendable warriors. (*David:* The work objects.) The machines that "take a licking and keep on ticking till our batteries wear down and we die."

So the thing is we get punished for that, of course, because we are work objects and we become work addicts. And we think that intimacy and loving equal working hard for someone. (Laughter.) That kills us, and it also keeps us from ever having intimacy, because the people

we want to have intimacy with are long gone after we
have worked so much.

Men's power is an illusion because all of the things that
seem to be about power are the things that kill us, that
cause us to lead lives of stress and be out of control. We
lose our life, we lose our reality, we lose our spirituality,
we lose our families, we lose everything. That's powerless.
So from our power comes our powerlessness.

They did a study on the "imposter syndrome." They
found that 78% of all professionals felt like imposters.

David: I don't know about that. Tell me about it.

Terry: Most professionals said they really felt like imposters and feared they might get caught.

David: I heard that from Pat Mellody. When I interviewed Pat, he said that when he became a major in the
Air Force, he felt like a 14-year-old major.

Terry: Right, that's that whole thing, see. It's the Plimpton effect. Everybody feels like they're faking it, but
Plimpton[3] actually did go out and fake it.

David: He made a profession of faking it.

Terry: Yes, that's right. See, most of the professionals
who were interviewed in that study were men. And men
do feel like they're boys. See, that's our felt sense of our
powerlessness, our felt sense of childhood that we have a
hard time embracing and integrating into adulthood. We're
non-integrated creatures, and we operate in childish ways
or we operate in ways brought on to us by a culture that
forces us into those power roles.

That's the polarization of co-dependency again. When
you don't have true identity, you tend to polarize. I think
that in the men's movement there's a lot of childishness,
and I think there are a lot of power issues. It's a political
movement as well. Sometimes I actually think that some of

the men's movement — the male bonding stuff — is like a
new form of the good old boy network with a different
name, different membership criteria and different stan-
dards. I still recognize a lot of the good that comes from it.

David: John Lee really addressed that in a sense by
saying that he was not about forming another Kiwanis or
Jaycees club, that he was about other kinds of things.

Terry: You get political men who have been raised and
acculturated in what they've been raised and acculturated
in and they're co-dependents who lack identity. And
they're going to polarize. You're going to have either the
childishness or you're going to get the political and the
power issues going.
  I like Robert Bly and I like his poetry. I don't know
exactly what he's doing in his workshops, so I can't really
comment on that part, but I think a lot of what men are
going into reinforces sex-role rigidity. We're not learning.
See, we need to learn from each other. We need to learn
from women. Women have been studying men longer than
men for one thing. (Laughter.) We need to learn about
people first, and then I think we can sort out more about
our gender identity.
  I don't think we understand co-dependency and the
issues around it. We don't have a definition yet. But I feel
like I understand what it is.

David: I liked your definition that "Co-dependency is
what happens to kids in a dysfunctional family."[4]

Terry: When we can't depend on people, we develop
dependency problems. We don't learn how to depend on
ourselves. So we become either very dependable or very
undependable.

David: We don't learn to be independent either, because
we don't have any self-valuing process.

Terry: Right. Well, we do learn independence. On the one hand, we learn enmeshment and denial of our dependency, but remember, the polarization is that when we lack something we go for it. So, if we lack a sense of separateness, we'll go for it to the extreme and we'll become independent. What we don't learn is interdependence[5]. That's the approach I'm trying to find, a healthy balance between dependency and independence.

An independent person is a co-dependent who doesn't act it out in relationships. They have no more identity than the co-dependent. They have just realized that they lose too much of themselves in relationships, so they don't shoot for it because they can't stand to lose themselves. That's actually a co-dependent who just doesn't act it out. Or, the polarization of the enmeshment is isolation.

David: That went a little fast for me. Do you want to recap?

Terry: Okay. If I'm isolated, if I'm alone, if I'm an independent kind of person, why am I? Because when I get close to people, I can't take care of myself. I get too scared. That anxiety and that absence of boundary is co-dependency. A lot of co-dependents swing from enmeshment to isolation, excessive dependency to independence.

Some stay in one place or the other, but it still comes from an absence of developmental formation, spiritual values, identity and self-awareness as human beings first, and as men and women also. So my thought is that we need more conferences where we talk about men's and women's issues together, with each other, to each other and about each other. We need more conferences to deal with the issues of the family.

Families aren't a man's family and a woman's family, families are families. The hurt and the relationship problems we have don't come out of men's issues and women's issues. That's the red herring, that's the bullshit that everybody focuses on and writes about. (*David:* Well . . .) Just a second, just a second.

If I can't have intimacy, it's not because I'm a man, not because I'm a woman. The way I act out my inability to have intimacy will come from the cultural reinforcement of what it is to be a man or a woman. If I can't have intimacy, I guarantee you that it's almost always a result of what I learned about people and myself in my family. If there was no one in my family who was real enough to get close to, if I didn't see intimacy modeled, if I didn't get enough affirmation to have a sense of self-intimacy (which we eventually call identity), I'm not going to find it elsewhere. And after 12 years of research in this, I found that men and women come from the same families. (Laughter.)

We've been hurting in the same way in our vulnerability and our pain. Our bottom-line issues are the same. When we have more recovery and acceptance of that, we'll be holding hands in our recovery with intimacy. Siblings in the same family, male or female, don't generally get along very well if it's a dysfunctional family. It's not because of the anger that they portray or a dissonance, it's because of the stored pain. I can't get close to you because I have too much stored pain.

My thought is that it's as if we're from the same family. We've been hurt in the same ways and because of our stored pain we can't hold hands. But with siblings in a family in recovery there's a beautiful thing that happens. I see the hurt child in you because I grew up with you, and that touches the hurt and the grieving I need to do. We have a healing process and a bonding process, and that's what I think we need to do in recovery. Men with women and men and women.

David: I find that real scary at the moment. That's partly because I have turned the focus on myself and my own recovery because I can deal with that right now. I can't deal successfully with bigger issues.

Terry: Right. That's why I believe in starting with same-sex therapists. I also really support same-sex groups. I was in a men's group for 18 months, and that's where I did a lot of my recovery. But it was co-facilitated by a man and a woman. If that woman hadn't been in there, I wouldn't have had the same level of recovery and trust about women.

I do think that men's issues need to be addressed. I just think that we need to be doing it together as hurt children coming from the same family.

David: This may seem like an off-the-wall question. It occurred to me that, for some men, breaking with the mother is similar to a break with addictions. Do you think that idea has any validity?

Terry: I think it has validity, but I think it's the mother's break with the child and the father's unavailability to the child that sets up addiction. In other words, addiction is about dependency. So when our dependency needs are denied or misused, we have dependency problems — or co-dependency, essentially. So they become chemical dependency, sexual dependency, food dependency, substance dependency. We become dependent on things, collecting, hoarding whatever, spending, intensity dependency, crime, gambling, sex, whatever.

I think it's more that the addiction comes out of the breakup with Mom. Men are taught a bill of goods about us abandoning Mom, that we break off with Mom. Essentially, it is that Mom uses the child sometimes. When the child leaves Mom, he or she feels abandoned by her, but they were used anyway. The bond was there for Mom, not for the child. When that bond is there for the parent instead of the child, the breakup really affects the dependency needs of the child.

And, yes, it is abandonment. There's abandonment when we're used. There's abandonment when the person is unavailable to us emotionally or physically. And this abandonment is the core of our intimacy struggles, our fear of intimacy and abandonment. So abandonment becomes the first issue in most therapy processes.

Many of us experience abandonment in a lot of different ways. We bond to survival figures, even abusive or absent ones. So even when we're being used or abused, we bond to them. When we leave and they suffer, we assume that we're breaking the bond.

David: Right. We take it on ourselves.

Terry: We're set up to leave Mom. It's interesting that daughters are set up to be abandoned by Dad. But males feel like they're abandoning Mom. It's a weird thing. This is the tendency in families. You find it true more often than not, but it won't be anywhere near close to all the time.

David: I read that in your book, *Broken Toys, Broken Dreams*, that flip of family roles — reality is the flip side of the way it looks. In fact, the mother or the father is using the child by depending on that child, so when the child grows up somewhere in the late teens and they leave the parent, either the mom or the dad, particularly the male leaving the mother, then the child feels like he's abandoning the parent. That just really rang true. That really hit the bell for me.

Terry: A lot of men say that to me. A lot of men have been set up to feel that, and I believe a lot of men have been used. Seduction of a child by a parent is the most powerful seduction. A mom's seduction of a male child sets up that male child to react in many of the same ways that an incest victim will react.

David: So that becomes covert incest.

Terry: Covert, emotional, role reversal.

David: Let me toss out this notion, and you can hit it any way you like. When a woman comes up to me and calls me a feminist and she's trying to be nice to me, complimentary and so on, I have taken to saying, "No, I'm not a feminist. I'm a conscious male." That's different.

Terry: I know, I don't like "feminism" because it's a gendered label.

David: Exactly, I don't need your gendered label. I have my own gendered label.

Terry: Yes. I'm trying to stay away from gender and labels. See, a part of my interdependency approach is that feminism needs to be re-labeled because it's not about "feminine," it's about "human." So, maybe you're a "humanist." (Laughter.)

David: Well, there have been humanists around forever.

Terry: That's right. That's why I think we need to go back to a humanist philosophy and then define genders.

David: There's a lot of watered-down Christianity that shows up as humanism.

Terry: Yes, there is. I don't mind if a humanist is Christian, Buddhist, Taoist or whatever. The thing is once we start to sort out and define our humanism, we need to look at the gender identity within it. I'm not opposed to it happening concurrently, but I feel my role is going to be to emphasize the interdependency, the concepts of earlier feminist literature that I want to learn from and the holding hands in recovery together.

But there are some other issues, and that is that I know I don't have a hard time playing, I know I don't have a hard time traveling and being around men or women. We see things out of our own paradigms and we see needs out of our own paradigms. I always say co-dependency is a prism. What you see depends on the angle that you look at it from, and the angle that you look at it from depends on the positions you've come from in your own life.

So a physician sees co-dependency as a stress-related illness. A developmental psychologist sees it as something else, and a marriage counselor sees something else. We see the needs about men's and women's issues from our own paradigms.

David: That's always true of any issue. I think, for example, that all this stuff about journalistic objectivity or scientific objectivity is bunk. I think that what's real is to be able to recognize your own biases, your own prejudices, and to recognize where you're coming from in terms of asking a question.

Terry: Yes, and to allow messages to come through you without those prejudices affecting the message, but having your own message that you tell your prejudices within. To me that's good writing.

David: Right. In reading around in your book, *Broken Toys, Broken Dreams,* I was most struck by your discussion of PTSD and the comparison between co-dependents and Vietnam vets. I've known a number of vets and I worked with Vietnam Veterans Against the War and the American Friends Service Committee during the war. So that rang a lot of bells for me.

Terry: I started working with the Vietnam Vets Family Project along with Jim Moffatt, the most highly decorated soldier in the history of the United States. He was a Black Beret in Vietnam, and there are only about two left out of the 100 they commissioned. All of them either died in combat or from cancer from Agent Orange. I learned a lot from Jim and Linda about what was happening in vets' families in the mid '70s and earlier. It began happening right away. I also realized in working with some of the vets that most of the ones with the most severe issues came from violent or alcoholic families. Then I saw the correlation between the adult children, the family members of the victims of sexual trauma and the Vietnam vets and the need for the same therapeutic processes. I think the vets taught us about what helps people change in the debriefing, in the gentle support and all this misdiagnosed stuff.

There are so many victims of trauma. I think we have to deal with the trauma, which to me includes high crime areas and poverty, sexual abuse, and the way we view children and treat them in our culture. That's the key issue for me. It's not a men's or a women's issue.

David: It's a children's issue.

Terry: Yes, it's a family issue, a cultural issue. Men are abused. We are taught about war, to play war, to be aggressive. We are taught the hunter role, but it's more like hunting each other in business, in politics. We're taught killing. We're taught that intimacy is sex. We're taught rape. We're taught that no doesn't mean no. Then we get in trouble when we act it out.

You see, when you have a sick system that teaches men all these things, you have identified patients. And the identified patients of our sick sexual system are the rapists who get busted for it, the victims of sexual molestation and abuse and the addicts. Those are the identified patients of our cultural illness.

In our culture, men who are the offenders are the identified patients more often than the victims. I think that's because men are acculturated not to recognize their victimization, not to talk about it and not to have more shame about it than the victim.

David: Right, that's one of the big changes that has come about with the program and the movement. Men have been able to see themselves as victims and to accept that.

Terry: We also have had a hard time owning our offender behavior, but there's less shame for some men in being an addict or an offender than in having been victimized. Whereas women will have more shame about being an offender than being a victim. So women have an easier time being recognized as a sexual abuse victim than a sex offender or addict.

That's why you'll see a lot more men identified as sex addicts. Of course, there's reinforcement. Men are taught that intimacy is sex, where women are taught that intimacy is affection. Women will become more love and relationship addicted.

David: They become love addicts. We become sex addicts.

Terry: Yeah, sex and work, love and relationships. But there's a lot of crossover because we're human beings.

I want to make a comment. I don't like the concept of the opposite sex. Other sex is preferable. In some ways, it's understandable how we keep getting reinforced for dealing with women as the opposite sex. Anyway, men get set up by being victims of the culture, of the family, and especially in sexual areas, sexual empowerment and male identity stuff.

David: I want to go back to the Vietnam vet question again. I'm remembering a comment that Bly made. He has a contention that in Korea and particularly in Vietnam, we lost our identity as warriors. He contrasts us with the Japanese, who underwent "total surrender" at the end of World War II. Yet they kept their warrior spirit enough so that now they're soldiers in the armies of Sony and Datsun and so on. Their warrior spirit has been maintained, and they're winning as soldiers in those armies.

It's Bly's contention that we've lost that warrior spirit, that sense of winning, and that we need to revive it in some way. Does that make any sense to you?

Terry: Actually, there's a lot of it that does make sense. What happens when you participate in something that is culturally shameful is that you lose your spirit. You lose your spirituality, because the shame is internalized and not dealt with, and it becomes a part of your identity. It's

like we hide our cultural shame in underground silos.
(Laughter.)

I would call it a competitive spirit, not a warrior spirit.
To compete is to do the best you can. To be competitive is
to have to beat someone down to feel better about yourself. Competitiveness comes out of shame as well, or poor
self-identity and the absence of boundaries. To be able to
compete comes out of a sense of pride. I can do my best
and I can go for winning, but I don't have to beat someone
else to feel good about myself.

We haven't lost our aggressiveness and there's a warlike,
if not warrior, mentality in our culture. Periodically we
have to invade some tiny country because even those mid-
dle-sized southeast Asian ones are too feisty now. So let's
hit Grenada and Panama? The tinier the better. It's too
bad that we own Rhode Island, because we could invade
that one and be okay.

David: What about Iraq? Have we bitten off more than
we can chew?

Terry: Well, of course, because we already can't win
there no matter what, because of our own track record,
our own history of mistakes and shameful aggressive behaviors. There's nothing that we can do there that will do
us much good. So we're in a bind there.

David: Unless we can get back that 20% of the world's
oil supply from Kuwait.

Terry: Yeah, it's about oil and oil prices, but even without
the oil issue there's not much we could do there that would
do us much good, but we're so committed and our world
is so interwoven that we have to be there. We set it up.

You know how co-dependents in the family will set up
the dynamics, and then they can't win. The addict actually
does that, too. Even when you're trying to be good, you
can't win. Even in recovery, it's like things have gone too
far, and you're just going to have to take a lot of shit for

a long time and the recovery will work itself out over a lot of time. It's a process. I think as a country we've done that.

Human systems are so complex and variable that I get scared when we try to put them in a box. I do, and a lot of other people in the field do. We describe the wind. So I've grown up in the city and I see the wind and what it does in the city. But, boy, it's a wholly different thing to a sailor. It's a wholly different thing to a person in a forest. It's a wholly different thing in the winter. (Laughter.) We always describe the wind and what we see the wind affecting, which is what's around us and again, through our paradigm.

David: And in terms of our warrior spirit in Vietnam...

Terry: Okay, the warrior spirit. Vietnam was a very complex issue, just like co-dependency is. It was the tolerance break of a co-dependent culture. It was acting out. It was the arrogance. It was the inability to realize we made a mistake. The Vietnam vets came back and they were traumatized because the war didn't seem to have any sense of meaningfulness. And meaningfulness is a core part of spirituality. So there was a spiritual breakdown in our culture that affected the entire culture. One-third of the homeless are Vietnam vets.

We haven't even looked at the PTSD echoes in the families of the vets and the friends of the vets. Our entire culture is echoing PTSD and has been since Vietnam. Incidentally, World War II vets had PTSD, too. It just didn't come up until later. The immediate effects of any trauma will be delayed if you can ascribe some meaningfulness to the trauma.

David: And then they'll surface later.

Terry: Generally later, much later sometimes.

David: You also brought up the example of the concentration camp survivor, where the survivor who felt there was some meaning to their going through this was able to handle the memory of the experience much more easily than somebody who . . .

Terry: Yes, and they were shattered when it was meaningless. Think about men's lives and how meaningless what we do is, overall. And think about women who have been involved in more value-oriented things, such as family, children. I'd say we need to network with each other in ways that have more meaning.

Men network better than women, but in meaningless ways — business, politics, sports. (Laughter.) Women network in more meaningful ways. Men's spirituality is becoming more shallow, because we haven't been providing enough meaning in our lives.

David: When I interviewed Ken Richardson he brought out what seemed to me a really core question in men's issues, or maybe anybody's issues, but men's for the moment because that's our immediate prism. It came in the form of a question that someone put to him. It went this way. "Think of your work, think of your family, think of your home, think of your animals, think of your hobbies. Lose all those, then who are you?" Ken said, "I'm nothing." The reply was, "See how you describe yourself." To me that's a key question in our lives.

Terry: As nothing . . . the shallowness of meaning in our lives.

David: Well, who are we once we take away the work, the family, and all that other stuff? It strikes me as a question women don't really ask themselves.

Terry: I wouldn't assume that, though. How many women have made men their meaning? When you take away the man, what's the meaning in their life? If their kids are their meaning, take away the kids? Their home, their meaning? Take away the kids and the furniture. Actually, men are just starting to ask it. Women have been asking it for a long time.

David: So we're back to the spiritual quest again. Once you start following that line of questioning . . .

Terry: We're back to the absence of real difference in men and women. It's just that men are slower in asking the questions, maybe.

David: To me, the feminist movement came out of questions like, "What's our value, and how can we establish value for ourselves?"

Terry: And being abused by men.

David: And being abused by men.

Terry: And that still goes on.

David: Oh sure.

Terry: But men are abused by men, and women . . .

David: The thing is that women started to abuse each other the same way that men have, and so now they get heart attacks . . .

Terry: Like you say, men are threatened by men. Well, we are because we're all competing. Some might say it's for women, and some might say it's for money, and some might say it's for masculinity, but we're all competing.

Women are threatened by women, too. When they get in the workplace, sometimes they're the meanest to each other. Women have a hard time having secretaries who are women. They try to find men secretaries. The issues are very similar.

David: My experience in the work world was that women were much tougher bosses than men.

Terry: Yes, and part of that is over-compensation, because they've been abused by the system so much in getting there that they've had to toughen up. Only the
tougher ones are going to make it, the intimidating ones,
because men in business don't respect a lot of feminist
values. Because business has been based on what we in
our gender descriptions call a masculine system.

There's something else, too. Men tend to blame their
anger on women and moms, but our anger at women is
really displaced anger at absent dads. I'm convinced of
that. In other words, we're born of women, we bond with
women, and we get angry at women so we can back off
and bond with Dad and develop male identity. But when
we don't find the male identity, we stay angry at women
and we lack male identity. (Laughter.)

Men's primary issue is a search for fathering. That's
why I say same-sex therapists because we need fathering
first.

David: That's the whole initiation question. (*Terry:* Yes.)
The benefit of initiation is that we get introduced into
what might be a successful role as a man.

Terry: Except that it's too late. Infants bond with caregivers who are close. It's not true that the survival bond
is a bond with Mom because of birth. It's true that Mom
is involved by nurturing and caring for the child.

Even the feeding, you know. We make more of the
feeding, but it's the touching, the closeness, the holding.
When men are able to bond with their infants, then their
infants will trust men and have respect for men. If the
infant is a son, that son will develop male identity from
that bonding. And out of their male identity, they will be
able to seek and find their roles.

It is an initiation to be able to bond with men, but it's
better if it takes place along the way. See, you and I can
find it now, but it's one hell of a lot harder for me to kinda
curl up in your lap and feel safe and small. I can do it, but
it's harder now. It's harder for me to let in the advice and

care and nurturing and warmth and sounds than if I were an infant, because now I'm jaded and I have a hard time trusting you. But I can do it now.

I can find the fathering, but I can't find a father any more. So the men's movement seems to me to involve a lot of men seeking fathering so they can find healthy male identities, so they can love themselves. Out of that, we can have intimacy with both men and women. Women need mothering. Women need to get mothering. So they need the same thing as men. Men need mothering to learn to love and respect and feel safe and trusting with women, but more of their identity comes from loving the self as a man, and that's from being loved by men.

The other thing is that men have a tendency to find a father, or a father figure, for a period of their lives. What almost always happens is that the father figure turns out to be too much like their original father, or they set the person up, or they project on that person, or the person can't meet their child dependency needs. I don't know if you got to that part in my book about child dependency needs. They're insatiable.

Okay, so if you're my father, but I'm in my child dependency needs that have never been met or grieved or dealt with, then you're never going to be able to fill them. And so I'm going to drive you away. Men, if they get needy, tend to drive men away. So it's finding fathering in different ways from different people that to me is the key part we can get out of the men's movement. And letting what is given be enough from men is the next part of that.

David: Whew! We're on this speeding train. It's great. (Laughter.) One figure or image or metaphor that's being tossed around a lot is the image of the Wildman or the Trickster or the Coyote. Can you think of a Coyote figure in your life, or a Trickster?

Terry: I'm only vaguely familiar with that concept. I know that I've seen it, but I haven't slowed down enough to process any of that part. I have men in my life, and I'll bet I could tie them into those roles, but I'm not exactly sure what each one represents.

David: Well, the Coyote takes on a different flavor depending on the culture. In Navajo or Hopi culture, the Coyote figure is evil. He's trouble. This is bad change.

Terry: I think there are an awful lot of male Coyotes in my life.

David: On the other hand, his simple existence gets your attention. He creates an awareness.

Terry: A lot of growth can come from the Coyote, but he can be like a nemesis, one who will trick you. Does he steal from you?

David: If you're weak, you'll fall victim to his tricks, and you lose out. If, on the other hand, you're aware and have strength, you can ride it.

Terry: Does the Coyote not pay his dues and steal a lot? Would that be a Coyote?

David: That happens. Bly, from Grimm[6], brings up the figure of the False Landlord, where the false landlord is the guy who steals the gold you've earned after a great deal of work.

Terry: Okay. Maybe that's the analogy. I worked very hard with some very brilliant people for a long period of time. It's like I paid my dues for years and years doing very long, hard weekends of teaching for minimal to no money. After 15 years of that, I had some payoffs. My work was cutting edge and sound. I think I added my own pieces to it. And in a very short time one person in my life came along and ran with it. He went through a workshop, got some tapes and ran with it. He became, you know, like multiples of success with that information. He credited me a bit here and there and then stopped when I started resenting what was happening. From that experience I had a bad year, some resentment, and then I decided finally to just do what I do because the information wasn't mine. It was learned and gleaned from others, and I added my part. So what happens with it will happen with it.

Boy, that was a tough one. Then I made a decision to change my life a great deal. I had some people in my life who were very close, one male in particular, and he over-reacted to my decision, didn't support me through my pain, and the lack of support cost me financially. I don't know what role that would be. But it felt like a Coyote, because I felt like I had been used the whole time. Tricked.

The latest case was maybe in the last eight months. I made a decision to leave a marriage, and it's amazing how none of the people that I thought I'd get support from supported me, or gave me any sense of support. They all questioned how I did it and why I did it. No one acknowl-edged the pain and the need I had for support from people I'd been working with for years at that time.

David: So all of a sudden you found yourself out there alone?

Terry: Well, one of the wonders of the 12-Step recovery programs is that you're never really alone. You've got those meetings, you've got that cause, you've got those people. I found out there were other people who I hadn't been very close to who were available, and so I could reach out. I didn't have a problem with isolation, I had a problem with grieving the people I thought were going to be there for me and weren't.

David: I experienced that, too. Since I went into recov-ery, I have lost touch with or been cut off from practically everybody I knew before, and I know new people in the program. I'm working. Here I am, I'm trying to lead a moderate life is what I'm trying to do.

Terry: I've had some male mentors in my life who were a profound influence on me.

David: You want to talk about them? That's a different category. Mentoring is one of the things that the men's movement has been advocating. In the past year, one of the most meaningful things that has happened to me was when I went to the Men and Co-Dependency Conference[7] in Phoenix. As part of the closing ceremony, they asked all the men who were 50 and over to join in a central circle. Then everybody celebrated us for the fact that we'd survived this long. And it was really wonderful to be honored in that way.

Terry: Well, there is a point where we gradually achieve wisdom if we have integrity, if we've done the integration work.

David: And part of the message was okay, now you can go and mentor the younger men through their process. I've now done that twice through two men's organizations. I find that very valuable.

Terry: In childhood my mentors gave me very little, almost nothing, but it was all I got from adults. And it was positive. And it had a profound impact.
I think the mentoring concept for the child who isn't getting that can have a profound impact on his life. One male teacher just said something to the effect that I was going to make something out of myself. A coach paid my fees and got my uniforms even when he wasn't coaching. Both of those experiences had a big impact on my life.

David: So even a small effort on the part of a male mentor turned out to have a profound effect.

Terry: To a child who is not getting the fathering, a man coming in and doing any semblance of fathering, no matter how insignificant or unintentional, will have a profound impact. Usually the child won't be able to acknowledge it or even realize it at the time, so it will go unnoticed. But it always has an impact.

Most of us minimize our impact on each other. Like you turn to a person sitting next to you and you smile, or you say something friendly, and it has a profound emotional impact on most people. You sneer at someone and that does too. You can make or break a person's day with just a glance. We have a profound impact on each other.

David: That's a little bit daunting, but true.

Terry: It's amazing, isn't it? It's a little bit co-dependent too, letting someone make or break your day with a look. (Laughter.) It might be gas. (Laughter.)

David: You certainly run a fast track. I know one of the other questions that I wanted to raise was about money.

Terry: Money is the male makeup kit.

David: Sure. The boys with the biggest toys . . .

Terry: That's our vanity. Women's vanity is just placed in different ways. Men's vanity is just as large. In fact, men's vanity about physical appearance is growing. Do you know that in the '60s and '70s most men were satisfied with their bodies? About half of women were. In the '80s, less than half of men were satisfied with their bodies. And an even smaller percentage of women are. So what's happening is that men are getting caught in that physical vanity, but we have always been caught in the vanity of power and economics. And the attractive men in our culture have always been wealthy men.

David: Well, I agree with you that money is not worth working for. In some ways, I always thought that. That's why I went into teaching originally.

Terry: That's what I did, too. That was my adolescent value. Then I got sort of caught up in it, because I loved toys and I love to play. I like old cars. I finally started discovering that you're owned by what you own. (Laughter.) And then I'm trying to own the world. So I like Frank Lloyd Wright's statement, "I've got this seashell collection, and you've seen it. I keep it scattered on beaches all over the world." (*David:* That's great.) Or my mother's statement, "You can't have everything. Where would you put it?"

David: Yes, my '56 Chevy convertible is out there somewhere. Who knows where?

Terry: I get to see it once in a while, though. (Laughter.)

NOTES

1. Second Annual National Conference on Co-Dependency, August 26-29, 1990, Scottsdale, AZ, U.S. Journal/Health Communications, Inc.

2. The First Step of Co-Dependents Anonymous (CoDA): "We admitted we were powerless over others — that our lives had become unmanageable." CoDA, P.O. Box 33577, Phoenix, AZ 85067.

3. George Plimpton is a writer and actor known for his impersonations, particularly for appearing as a literary man in professional sports scenarios.

4. Terry Kellogg with Marvel Harrison, **Broken Toys, Broken Dreams,** BRAT Publishing, Amherst, MA, 1990.

   Contact BRAT Publishing for earlier tape series of Terry on the following subjects and others: Sexuality and Intimacy, Spirituality, Family Roles, Feelings and Physical Stress, Relationships and Shame.

5. Terry has been developing the concept of interdependence with Marvel Harrison. Their new book, **Finding Balance, 12 Priorities for Interdependence and Joyful Living,** Health Communications, Inc., Deerfield Beach, FL, 1991, presents this concept in detail. See also *Changes,* January 1991.

6. Robert Bly, **Men and the Wound,** Minnesota Men's Conference, October 12, 1985. Human Development Association, Milwaukee, WI.

7. Conference on Men, Relationships and Co-Dependency, April 1990, Phoenix, AZ, U.S. Journal/Health Communications, Inc.

MIKE LEW

MIKE LEW

Mike Lew's book *Victims No Longer: Men Recovering from Incest and Other Sexual Child Abuse* offered the first comprehensive description of childhood sexual aggression and recovery for the male victim. In doing this pioneering work, Mike chose to address the deepest wound a male child can experience. He points out that at least one adult male in four has been sexually abused before he reaches the age of 18. He is supported by Pat Carnes[1] who indicates that in the research population for his new book, *Don't Call It Love*, 80% of both the men and women surveyed had been sexually abused before reaching the age of 18!

Mike chose to work with a human problem that few people wanted to look at with clear, compassionate and open eyes. Mike sets the social problem for the male survivor with clarity on the cover of his book:

Our culture provides no room for man as victim. Men are simply not supposed to be victimized. A "real man" is expected to be able to protect himself in any situation. He is also supposed to be able to solve any problem and recover from any setback. When he experiences victimization, our culture expects him to "deal with it like a man."

Mike is co-director of The Next Step Counseling and Training Center in Newton Centre, Massachusetts. He has focused on developing strategies for recovery from incest and other abuse, particularly for men. In addition to working with clients, Mike conducts workshops and lectures for mental health professionals throughout the United States and Europe.

Mike completed the course work for a Ph.D. in psychological anthropology at Columbia University and was an assistant to Margaret Mead. He has taught at the City College of New York and other institutions. His education allows him to bring a cross-cultural approach to his work. He is a member of numerous professional organizations.

Personally, Mike is an engaging man who demonstrates a clear sense of humor, at the same time that he is clear and focused in his approach to his subject. When I interviewed him, he chose to come to my office on his way to conduct a training. Even though I had sent him a set of topics that we might discuss, it was clear from the outset that he had his own agenda. And that was fine. His extraordinary compassion for wounded men and women pervades his view of humanity.

INTERVIEW WITH
MIKE LEW

August 22, 1990 • Albuquerque, New Mexico

David Lenfest: Of all the books I've read in the recovery field, the two that absolutely transfixed me, that I literally could not put down, were Pat Carnes' *Out of the Shadows*[1] and your book, *Victims No Longer*[2]. When I was reading your book, my reaction was "This guy's been reading my mail." (Laughter.)

Mike Lew: I have heard that. One of my colleagues said he didn't think I wrote the book, he thinks I channelled it because I seem to have tapped into something for a lot of people. I don't think that this book really did come out of me. In a very real sense, I think the book came out of my ability to listen to what the male survivors, my clients and the other male survivors I was meeting, were saying [n.b.: He refers here and throughout the interview to male survivors of child-

129

hood sexual abuse.], and to be able to translate that in a way that other people could hear.

David: Well, it certainly makes a lot of sense. You have a statement on page 42 which I found . . .

Mike: You've probably read the book better than I have! (Laughter.)

David: . . . Remarkable. You say, "Similarly, he (the survivor) devalues his strength and power because he alone knows how weak and defenseless he feels. Whether his strengths, power and successes are physical, financial, professional, romantic, sexual, emotional, athletic, academic, intellectual or social, he finds cause to write them off. *No picture of reality is able to penetrate his wall of self negation"* (my emphasis).
I thought that a remarkable statement.

Mike: That came from my approaching this field with tremendous respect and admiration for the survivors. I'm talking now about the male survivors, because I work predominantly, overwhelmingly, with men. Here are people who successfully negotiated the most difficult of shoals. The very first task as I see it, the primary task of a child who's being abused, is to *get through* the abuse of childhood, to survive it any way that he or she can.
They're doing this in an environment where they have limited information, limited experience with the world, misinformation and lies — because sexually abusing a child is lying to him. It's lying to him about the nature of reality, the nature of caring, of love, of protection, of intimacy and many other things. Faced with all of this and often with brutal violence on top of it, the task for a child to figure out a way to get through this childhood is a statement of tremendous creativity, courage and intelligence. I see these adult men still feeling like scared little children, feeling incomplete, damaged, useless, all these negative things.

Here are men who needed tremendous creativity, tremendous intelligence, tremendous capability, simply to have survived. And what they were doing was negating that tremendous accomplishment. Nobody can begin to recover while they're still fighting simply to survive. I shouldn't say simply because it's not simple.

Nobody can begin a recovery process until they've established a sense of safety, enough time and distance from the abusive situation, enough real safety. I'm not talking about comfort here, because recovery is not a comfortable process. But it needs to be safe. Survivors need to know that they're not being abused further. Just as one can't get sober while drinking, one can't recover from sexual child abuse while being abused or while abusing another person.

David: Okay, that's very clear. Is it fair to extrapolate, to say that the man who was sexually abused as a child and who has overcome it is in some sense a leader? He became an adult, perforce, very early in the game.

Robert Bly, for example, talks a lot about men being hunters. He has a paradigm of a hunter as a way of a man finding himself, identifying himself and relating to nature. It's almost as if the people you're talking about are hunting for themselves. "Who am I?" seems to be the question.

Mike: Oh, there's certainly a search for self. I wouldn't use the word "hunter," though. Let me backtrack. I was doing a training a while ago at the Brattleboro Retreat in Vermont, and one of the participants came up to me and said he would like me to present a typology of the male incest survivor. I caught my breath, and then I laughed.

We're talking about the possibility of one in four men having been severely abused before the age of 18. Therefore, the only typology is one of diversity. I don't think we can fairly encapsulate the personality of the incest survivor. We're talking about maybe one in four children who will be severely abused before the age of 18, boys and girls, males and females.

David: That's a staggering number.

Mike: It is staggering. And so the only typology is one of diversity. I continually hear from survivors, both male and female, statements like, "I feel as though I never got the rule book." "Everybody else seems to know what they're doing." "I'm just trying to figure the world out." Clients will say to me again and again, "Do you understand me?" "Do you know what I mean?" "You're going to think I'm crazy." "This may sound crazy, but . . ."

I used to think this was a figure of speech like somebody saying, "You know?" But it is a reality. People didn't get the correct information.

David: They didn't get any feedback.

Mike: They didn't get any feedback, or the feedback they got was lies. They're trying to figure out what sane behavior is by extrapolating from an insane childhood. So when someone asks me a question like that, I take it very seriously. I say, "Yes, I understand." "No, that doesn't sound crazy to me." Or, "I don't understand this part. Would you explain this further?" And I find myself saying, "No, you're not crazy. What happened to you was crazy. Sexually abusing a child is crazy, and you are not sexual abuse. Sexual abuse is what happened to you. You're not responsible for it."

David: You're not the insult.

Mike: No, you're not the insult. And people do confuse themselves. They define themselves in terms of what happened to them. It's essential for adult survivors to move to the point where they can separate who they are from what was done to them.

David: At that point, they're beginning to enter the edge of what's supposed to be the general population. They're coming — to steal the term from Pat Carnes —

from out of the shadows, and going into whatever the central population is, which is also one of our questions. I'm wondering if this isn't a truly perverse male initiation?

Mike: How do you mean?

David: Well, if it's one in four, it's an initiation into being a man for one-fourth of the men out there.

Mike: If it's one in four females as well, I don't think it's a specifically gender-based initiation. We're certainly getting more and more reports of female perpetrators. I spoke to a member of the executive board of one of the national incest survivor organizations, one of the anonymous organizations, and she said that now they're getting about equal numbers of reports of female perpetrators by both female and male survivors.

Now I don't know if this means there are equal numbers of female perpetrators, but it certainly means there are significant numbers. I think the quest for both male and female survivors is to understand that recovery doesn't mean that you walk blithely into danger.

The world is neither a completely safe nor a completely dangerous place. One of the primary goals of recovery is to be able to determine what is safe and what is dangerous, to figure out how one learns whether he's in danger from another human being or from a particular situation. We're not always walking into dangerous situations, but we're not always avoiding any kind of social interaction for fear of abuse. That's a difficult problem if one is coming from an abusive environment.

David: It certainly is. I'm just trying to think about how to track this, because we're approaching it from a different point of view. I mean, your perception of men seems to be that of a group of people who are fundamentally wounded. You're starting from the wound and moving outward, whereas a lot of other people seem to be starting with a presumption of some kind of wholeness or health.

Mike: No, no. I don't agree. I don't think I'm starting from that perspective at all. A human child is born with an infinite capacity for love and zestful appreciation of life and creativity and intelligence and playfulness and caring and intimacy and all of those things. Abusing a child is saying to the child that none of those innate characteristics is valid.

What a child learns is a culture of abuse. He learns that the world is a dangerous, frightening, abusive place. If anything, the fact that anyone survives an abusive childhood is testimony to the innate strength, creativity and intelligence of human beings, male and female. I don't see men as wounded, and I don't see women as wounded. I see wounds as what happens to people. And people need to recover from these wounds in order to recapture and reclaim their essential humanness.

I usually tell a story at the end of each training, but I won't save it for the end now. Back in my last career, I was teaching cultural anthropology.

David: Where were you teaching?

Mike: I started teaching at the City College of New York. I also taught at the College of New Rochelle, but later I was teaching at a small college in Connecticut. I was also teaching at a maximum-security state prison. I was very popular among my colleagues because I'm a morning person, and I would volunteer to take all the eight o'clock classes if they wouldn't make me take the four o'clocks. (Laughter.) Everyone was very happy with me. They could sleep late. I would come home in the afternoon and turn on the television set and watch reruns of the Waltons. (Laughter.)

I would watch these reruns with tears running down my face, and I knew it wasn't the quality of the acting or the quality of the scripts particularly. I didn't understand at the time why I was crying, and I think I do now. What I was watching in these programs was people continually reaching for one another's essential humanity. They didn't always get it right. They didn't always make it. But they kept trying to touch what was essentially human in the other individuals in the show. Whenever I see something like that, it moves me tremendously.

I see that continually in the male and female survivors I work with, that I listen to, that I learn from. I see it in the professionals who are working in child abuse recovery, because I never met a more special bunch of people, many of whom are survivors themselves. Whenever I see people reaching for that humanity, I see it as world-changing. I see it as earth-shaking, and it moves me to my core.

David: That's interesting. A lot of what I've been doing in this interviewing is making gender distinctions, trying to make distinctions between how men experience themselves, how they experience their own growth, how they experience their changes.

Let me try a question on you that occurs to me. It seems to me that for a man the break with the mother is similar to a break with addictions. Bly asserts that the male ego is weak and he implies that this weakness leaves him attached to Mom and his addictions. Do you think there's any validity in that?

Mike: I don't approach things in as gender-based a fashion as that. I begin with humanness. I don't see a whole lot of evidence of tremendous differences between the genders that are not culturally based and culturally determined and learned behavior. I see far more similarities than differences in the experiences of female and male survivors of abuse. The differences that are there come largely from our cultural expectations about men and women, boys and girls, our culture-based understanding of abuse and what it is to be masculine or feminine.

There's a lot of confusion in the male survivor's experience, because we don't have a place in our culture for the victimization of men. We expect men to be able to handle themselves, to take care of themselves in any situation and to respond "like a man," which all too often means to forget about the abuse or to respond violently. Unfortunately, there's a lot of room at the bottom, and we don't have to create artificial distinctions about whose experience is worse — male or female, gay or heterosexual, older or younger — at the time the abuse took place.

I'm only speaking about sexual abuse recovery, because that's what I know about. I can't speak to a universal male condition. I don't know that there is one. Initially, all of the pioneering work in sexual abuse identification, recovery, treatment and healing was done by women, specifically by feminist therapists working with women. They created the safety for male survivors to begin to work on their own recovery.

Now we've reached a point where we can no longer depend on women to do our work for us. It's not right. It's not fair. It's not reasonable. We have to come to an understanding of what men have to do together to support one another in healing and recovery. One of the things incumbent upon us to do is to show our appreciation of the pioneering work women have done by not creating false distinctions, by not saying that male recovery is more important or that the abuse of males is worse than that of females. Rather, we need to support women in the work they're doing. At the next national conference on male sexual abuse[3] Laura Davis[4] and I are planning to do a session for the whole conference called "Can We Talk?" on bringing the male and female survivor/recovery movements together.

David: Well, what underlies my question is a perception that a lot of men remain involved with their mothers in one way or another, and that they don't separate.

Mike: Or their fathers.

David: Well, the mother particularly. The paradigm is that the mother is protective in some way or another, nurturing, and the father is the abusive alcoholic.

Mike: That hasn't been my experience in my life. (*David:* Nor mine.) That may be a theoretical paradigm, but I don't think it holds true when you listen to people's life experiences. There's father. There's mother. There are all kinds of significant others, depending on the family and the ethnic and cultural environments.

Initially when men responded to feminism, many thinking and caring men responded out of guilt and shame. They recognized that women had been oppressed, and they took on personal responsibility for it and ended up feeling bad about being male. What the men's movement in the best sense has been trying to do is to recognize the fact that nothing positive comes from guilt and shame.

Growth comes from a determination to take responsibility and make changes, not to sit around wallowing in guilt or shame or resentment. For a while, there was a kind of counter-reaction, a counter-rigidity to the guilt and shame, the equivalent of feminist separatists. There have been male separatists who have been trying to get their own strength, their own sense of self-esteem back by going overboard in the other direction. I think the image of a warrior is a necessary movement overboard in the other direction. But ultimately it's not the direction that men need to take.

David: Well, ultimately we're going to get integrated. I think the question a recovering man has to ask himself is where he is on this continuum, in this progress. What does he need at this particular point to move him the next step along the line? It's a mistake for people to assume that they can get to integration without taking the steps.

Mike: I think there are different times when people need different steps. You're absolutely right. Just as there was a real necessity for women at a certain point in their growth, and there still is, to be in all-female environments and to work with only women. I think this is also true for many men at points in their growth, their change, their healing and their quest for self-understanding. We do need

to not depend on women for our growth and our person-
hood. We have to learn how to interact with one another
in caring, supportive and genuine ways.

David: Right, and that we can support each other as
men emotionally. We don't need necessarily to look to
women for that.

Mike: Absolutely. This is one of my pet soapboxes.
There's a tremendous amount of misinformation around
about the nature of emotions and the expression of emotions. It's culturally based, because every culture defines
what's appropriately male and female.
   First of all, we have a mythology that women have
access to their emotions and men don't. That is a myth,
and it's a dangerous one. The reality is that we allow
women the expression of those feelings that we define as
legitimately female, and we allow men the expression of
those feelings that we define as legitimately male. For
women, it's the emotions that express fear and grief, crying, shaking. Men are not supposed to be scared. Men are
not supposed to cry. Men are traditionally allowed one
single emotional agenda — rage, anger. Men are allowed
to express anger, and women are not supposed to. So
women are kept from the full range of expression of emotions, too.
   Also, men are allowed to express gutsy enjoyment more
freely than women. (*David:* Gusto.) Gusto. Right, it's a
male image. (Laughter.) What this does is keep both men
and women from access to the full range of human emotion. I fault therapists, many therapists, who have a single
emotional agenda. It usually takes the form of something
like this, "You really need to get in touch with your . . .,"
and then they fill in their pet emotion. "You really need to
get in touch with your rage. You really need to get in
touch with your grief." When I hear this, I hear the therapist saying, "I really need to get in touch with my rage,
and I wish you would show me how to do it." (Laughter.)

The reality is that what the human needs to get in touch with is whatever feelings are there. We're complex beings. We're not sea slugs. We're capable of feeling several emotions at once, seemingly conflicting. We're capable of feeling anger and joy and grief and confusion at the same time. We can do that. It's not really a paradox. And that's what we need to do. We need to cry as much as we need to cry and stop crying when we're finished, and then maybe do something else. We need to rage in an appropriate manner, a nonviolent, non-hurtful manner, as much as we need to.

Often some other feeling comes up behind the rage. Sometimes that's grief, sometimes fear, sometimes relief or it's a combination. And we need to do this for as long as we need to do it.

David: That's good and that correlates interestingly enough with the kind of stuff that John Lee, for example, is doing from the Austin Men's Center. His book, *The Flying Boy*, has sold 60,000 copies, and he celebrates there his ability to cry and to grieve and to go through a whole range of emotions. But in particular, it's okay for him as a man to cry.

Mike: It's more than okay. It's absolutely necessary. I talk about tears as the lubricant that healing moves forward on. One of my colleagues, Janet Yassen, talks about 1,500 hours of crying as being a minimum for recovery. (Laughter.) She's not saying that so people will start their timers, but rather to indicate that this is a long-term process. It doesn't happen overnight. And men, of course, learn to fix things. They want to find quick solutions, get things done and move on. Sometimes things don't happen that way.

The other part of the piece on emotions is that what I get very frequently from men is fear of expressing their emotions as a fear of loss of control. And it gets worded as, "If I start to cry, I'll go crazy," or "I'll never stop." "If I get angry I'll kill somebody," or "I'll kill myself."

David: Sure, there's a raging homicidal maniac underneath this . . .

Mike: It's a fear of that. It comes from their experience of violence and their experience that anger leads to violence. Anger is a feeling. Violence is a behavior. It's one possible expression of anger, but it's not the only possible expression. My experience has been that people don't go crazy from crying. They go crazy from not being able to express their feelings, from having their feelings stifled, from stuffing them. When men begin to cry, they cry until they've cried enough. Then they stop crying, and they do something else.

At some other point, they may have more tears coming up. When men get angry and have adequate, healthy, nonviolent expressions of their anger, they rage as long as they need to rage, and then they stop raging. And often something else comes up behind it. Usually in my experience that's been either fear or grief, or some combination of the two. But they don't go out and kill somebody unless they don't have legitimate, nonviolent channels for their anger. And so what we have to do is not cap people's anger.

Survivors need to rage, but they need to have healthy outlets so they don't have to be afraid of their feelings whatever their feelings are. They need healthy outlets so they can express their feelings in a way that leads to healing and recovery rather than leading to further abuse of themselves or another person.

The other thing that's essential to look at is shame and humiliation. John Bradshaw[5] talks beautifully about the nature of shame, and many other people do as well. I think it's difficult to understand the depth and the intensity of the shame that male survivors carry about their experience. And it's essential that they talk about how ashamed and humiliated they feel.

I've met many male survivors who need to talk about their humiliation fantasies, even their acting out of humiliating experiences sexually, either as the person who is humiliated or who does the humiliating or both. Men carry tremendous shame about having fantasies about humiliation.

David: Well, yes. They carry both sides of it, the victim and the oppressor.

Mike: Virtually all male survivors have heard the stereotype, the incorrect stereotype, that boys who are abused will grow up to become abusers. This is simply not so. The idea comes from a turning around of the understanding that most people who are abusers were themselves seriously abused as children. Not necessarily sexually, but somehow badly abused.

People turn that around and assume that someone who was sexually abused as a child will automatically grow up to be an abuser. My experience has been that the overwhelming number of men who were sexually abused grow up to become protectors in one way or another.

David: That's interesting.

Mike: We have a traditional role in our culture of woman as nurturer, mother. We don't have that for men. You find, I think, for that reason, an over-representation of male survivors in the human services, in the helping professions, in child protective work, in teaching.

David: They're all into nurturing in one form or another.

Mike: Nurturing and protection, law enforcement, prison work. They've said to themselves, often unconsciously, "I know what it feels like to have been abused, and I'm going to do everything I can to make sure that no child around me experiences that."

Many men come into treatment for their sexual abuse histories when they're about to become fathers, or when their child nears the age that the father was when he was abused. They'll say something like, "I don't want to do this. I don't want to look at these things. I don't want to feel these feelings. I don't want to have these memories, but I'll do anything to keep from abusing my child." I think these are statements of tremendous courage. If I say, "Do you feel like abusing your child?" the answer is almost always, "No."

"But I read somewhere that . . ." Or, "Isn't it true that . . ." Or, "I heard . . ." And then you get this old stereotype. "People with a history of abuse have training in abuse. That's why some percentage will become abusers — because that's what they have learned. That's where their training is."

David: It takes a major conscious effort to overcome that abusive training and go into nurturing.

Mike: The questions that get asked boil down to one set, and that is, "What does the fact that I was abused as a child mean about me? What is the significance of this key experience in my life? What does that mean about my masculinity?" This is, I think, part of the shame cycle that every male survivor asks himself. "Why me? Why did this happen to me and what does this mean about me?"

We've got to remember that abuse takes place in isolation. A child who's being abused frequently thinks he's the only child this is happening to. It happens in secrecy and in silence. Growing up, he doesn't know that this is happening to millions of other kids, so he asks, "Why me? Why did this person pick me?"

If the abuser was male, a male survivor will ask, "Does this mean that I'm really gay?" A heterosexual man will say, "Why did this person hone in on me? Is there something gay about me that I'm trying to repress or block? Even if I've never felt same-sex attraction, why did this happen to me?" So part of recovery for a heterosexual male survivor is exploring those fears of homosexuality and also, on a larger level, fears of intimacy, fears of intimacy with men, fears of intimacy with women.

The way a gay man asks the question is, "Is this what made me gay?" Or, "Did this happen to me because I'm gay?" If people are carrying a lot of internalized self-hatred or homophobia, they may even want this to be what made them gay because they think that if they find a cause there is hope of a cure.

We have no evidence of a causal link between sexual abuse of children and adult homosexuality. If there was such a link, you'd expect to find significant differences between male and female perpetrators, male and female victims and so forth. And there don't seem to be any. Often, when gay men explore their own histories, they reluctantly come to the conclusion that their same-sex attractions predated the abuse.

The other question, which I think is a much more significant and important question, is, "Did this happen to me because I'm gay?" And I think in a very specific sense that has to be understood. (You have to think about this carefully because it's open to misinterpretation.) The answer to this question is, "Yes." We have very specific culturally-based, gender-based expectations about how little boys and little girls should be, should appear, should speak, should behave. What activities they should be interested in. And any child, particularly any male child, who departs from our expectation of how a little boy should be is more likely to be treated abusively. That is, not if a child necessarily is gay, but if a child appears to be gay, effeminate, creative, emotional, academic, pretty, not interested in sports, nonviolent and on and on, he is at greater risk of abuse.

That is, if a little boy doesn't behave and look and sound the way we want a little boy to be, people take that as license to behave abusively toward him. I think this is true of little girls as well, but particularly true of little boys, and I think this is a tremendous tragedy. We don't honor diversity.

David: That means that, culturally, little boys have a much narrower frame of being that is considered appropriate. And if they're outside that framework, all of a sudden this is perceived as not being appropriate.

Mike: Right. It is perceived as something that has to be beaten out of them.

David: To be victimized?

Mike: Or they're perceived as less valid human beings, so it's okay to abuse them. This is a tremendous tragedy. It interferes with our wonderful human capacity for diversity. We should be thrilled with the fact that human beings are diverse. Little boys are all kinds of people. Little girls are all kinds of people. Until we value that, we're going to go on abusing our own children, the weakest and most vulnerable members of our society.

David: The other men I've interviewed seem to have gone along pretty much with my gender bias and worked their way around it. You're the first person to have just said, "No, No." (Laughter.) "Let's throw this gender bias out the window and talk about people, talk about 'us'."

Mike: I think that's vital. It doesn't mean we have to ignore that there are differences in a male and female experience. There may be innate differences, biochemical or genetic differences, but I think we must proceed from an assumption of basic humanness, basic humanity.

David: I think part of my interest, too, is that the women are so far ahead of us in being able to identify issues that they see as particularly feminine or endemic to women. The whole sociology, anthropology and even history of women's experience has become quite clearly defined, and that's very helpful for them. I don't think we quite have a parallel to that. We might have battles, dates and kings, but that isn't ordinary male experience.

Mike: So much comes from our experience, from our environment. I see a little boy or a little girl, and I see a child. I don't see a male or a female. You see a baby and you want to protect and nurture it, regardless of whether it's wearing pink or blue.

David: Another idea I want to talk about is this notion that men are acculturated to be work heroes or work objects, in somewhat the same way that women are acculturated to be sex objects. I wonder how you feel about that idea?

Mike: I think that's absolutely true. Although it's changing somewhat, it hasn't changed significantly in the culture at large. When we look at which of our clients have sexual abuse histories, one of the things we look at is addictions and compulsions, obsessive behaviors. It's very easy to recognize the addictions and compulsions and obsessions that are censured by society — the alcoholics, the drug addicts and the eating disorders. Presently, eating disorders are an interesting focus, because they used to be thought of as women's issues. In sexual abuse recovery, we see more and more male anorexics and male bulimics. It's becoming clear that this is not a gender based issue, it's an issue of abuse.

Beyond those things and the sex addictions and compulsions and the spending and debting and so forth, we find the addictive and compulsive behavior that gets rewarded by society. These tend to be more male-defined activities like workaholism, compulsive body-building, compulsive athletics and ultra-marathon running. These activities get rewarded by society. People who win marathons get money and laurel wreaths. Workaholics get defined as good providers and pillars of their communities, so they get that affirmation for numbing strategies that focus attention away from the abuse. And no one gets to see the isolated, frightened child hiding behind the bulging biceps or the BMW and the three-piece suit.

David: So it's a numbing strategy?

Mike: Oh, absolutely. We've got to be clear on this. None of the behaviors we're talking about is dangerous in moderation. There's nothing wrong with a glass of wine. There's nothing wrong with food or hard work or exercise. There's nothing wrong with sex. What we have to look at is the way these activities are being used. If they're being used compulsively and obsessively to the exclusion of healthy human interaction, they're being used to press down feelings.

With any of these things, if you need more and more medication to numb the pain, it becomes a problem. All of these behaviors initially were survival strategies. They were things that the hurting child, in the absence of other resources, figured out to numb the pain enough to get through the abusive experience to a time where he could begin a recovery process.

It's a survival strategy, and the child or the adolescent or the adult survivor deserves nothing but admiration and respect for figuring out something that would get him through it. It's only later in adulthood when these same strategies don't work as well, when the person needs more and more of the medicine to numb the pain and it's not working to numb the pain, that the strategy becomes a problem. The issues surface when they get in the way of healthy human interactions, satisfying career choices, healthy and non-abusive intimacy, friendships and closeness. When those numbing techniques get in the way of a healthy integrated life, they become problems. Then the person has to look for something else, and that something else, unfortunately, means bringing up all those painful feelings.

Nobody is going to give up a strategy that has worked, however badly. (Laughter.) Unless they're pretty sure they have something else that's going to replace it. That's why it doesn't make any sense to say to a drunk, "Well, you've got to stop drinking." They can't hear that.

David: Right. Just have one martini. (Laughter.) You deal with a population that has been damaged and tricked. There's a lot of talk in the men's movement about the validity of the wildman or the trickster or the coyote to bring a man around to a process of maturation. It seems to me that none of that really applies to the population you work with.

Mike: As I say, the population I work with is very diverse. I'm always suspicious of anybody who advocates a single path of healing or recovery. We're diverse, and there are many paths that work. People have different needs at different points in their recovery. The insistence that there's only one way to get through something is a path that leads to an abuse of power. "I am the way." Whoever says that is making, at best, a mistake. At worst, they're being manipulative and abusive.

There are many ways. Your book and the men you interview in it will certainly be evidence that there are many paths to understanding. There are many paths to healing. I'm rather suspicious of anyone who sets him or herself up as having the answer. I have far more questions than I have answers. When people cast me as expert, it doesn't sit well on my shoulders. Because to me the genuine experts are the survivors that I listen to and learn from and my colleagues in the field, many of whom have been doing this work far longer than I have. The time that I stop learning from survivors is definitely the moment for me to stop doing this work.

David: Right. I see that. It fits with the notion that when I stopped learning from the students, when I stopped having an interaction with students, was the point at which I stopped teaching. I realized I was burning out. I needed to go someplace else.

Mike: Exactly. We can learn in all sorts of ways. Certainly, we can learn from the wisdom of other cultures. You talked about the trickster, which is a Native American tradition, a Native American way of understanding. We have much to learn from Native Americans, just as we have much to learn from Eastern thought. But we also need to understand that we have much to learn from our own cultural traditions. If we're European/American, it's a mistake to reject European traditions. If we're African/ American, it's a mistake to reject African traditions.

There's so much to understanding. I think it's a mistake to say that we have to be somebody we're not, that we have to adopt something that's foreign in order to come to an understanding of humanness. There's tremendous diversity in the world, and we have to learn from our own histories as well as from the histories of others and be respectful of other people's histories.

David: As a culture, one of our habits, one of our traditions, has been absorbing other cultures. If you look at ethnic jokes in recent times, they start up being Irish, then they become Italian, then they get to be Polish and they're the same jokes.

Mike: There is also the same fear and distrust of other ethnicities under the guise of accepting them. Again, what I'm pushing for is diversity, not uniformity, whether we're talking about men or humans or ethnicity or race. What we need to cherish is our diversity and our complexity.

David: As far as you're concerned, then, there is no specifically male path?

Mike: I hope not. (Laughter.) I hope there are many male paths available to us. When we talk about sexuality, when we talk about sexual orientation, I think we have far more complexity, far more diversity available to us than, "This person is gay and this person is straight." I think we're just at the beginning of our understanding of sexuality. We won't come to understand it by limiting our perspective. We come to understanding by broadening our perspective. I think we're well on our way to doing that. And we've learned a lot from women about how to do that.

David: Let's close with one last question. Could you think of a list of needs, wants and characteristics that are possible for the adult male in the '90s?

Mike: My wish list? I would wish that we, as men, could learn not to try so hard, not to feel we have to have all the answers and to be the problem solvers. I wish we could learn better how to listen. And I wish we could move through some of our guilt and shame and fear to allow freer range of our emotions.

One of the things I see that's very encouraging, and I wish to encourage, is that we move past artificial distinctions, particularly around sexual orientation. We're beginning to see that gay men and heterosexual men and bisexual men and people who don't want to define themselves in terms of sexual orientation at all are beginning to see one another as natural allies and forge alliances with one another.

When I started doing groups for male survivors, I initially did separate gay and heterosexual groups. Now I only do mixed groups. Because what I see happening profoundly is gay and heterosexual and bisexual men coming to the understanding that we're not dealing with an issue of sexual orientation, we're looking at issues of sexual abuse of children. It's a tremendous cutting through of isolation for gay men to feel heard and supported and cared about by heterosexual men, for heterosexual men to feel heard and supported and not threatened by gay men. This is a tremendous piece of understanding that can only lead to an increase in our capacity for intimacy with women, with other men, with children — non-sexual, non-abusive intimacy.

It's only to the good when we break down these truly arbitrary barriers to our humanity. We can only do that when we begin to respect diversity. So my wish for the '90s is that we become more and more diverse, that we honor and value and celebrate our diversity and not feel that we have to carve out little territories, little turfs, and then protect and defend them.

The more it's okay for me to be exactly who I am, the more I can allow you that same respect.

David: Oh, exactly. I support that 100%. One of the revelatory experiences of this year, if not of the past 50 for me, was going to the Men and Co-Dependency Conference[6] in Phoenix. At the end of the conference they gathered all the men over 50 in a circle in the center and honored us as elders of the tribe, just for having survived over 50 years. Then I did a Wildman's Weekend with John Lee and Marvin Allen in the Ocate wilderness in New Mexico and they did the same thing, only in a more elaborate way.

They had the elders cross a line and be welcomed by Marvin and John, and then we formed up on two lines and we welcomed all the younger men as they came through as brothers in the tribe. (*Mike:* Yes, both have to happen.) We all became brothers in the tribe together. And that was just terrific.

Mike: This is my 50th year, and I'm just thrilled at what age brings. One of my heroes is a woman named Fay Honey Knopp. She's the head of the Safer Society Program[7]. She's been working in prisons for 50 years. She's a social worker, and she's a wonderful person. She did the wrap-up of the First National Conference on Male Sexual Abuse in Minneapolis a couple of years ago.

She's a very little woman with a shock of white hair. At the time she was 70. And she got up on the podium and she said, "I'm a social change agent. I'm an activist, and I advise you all to get grey." (Laughter.) "It took me 70 years to get to look like this and now I can get away with murder." (Laughter.) She proceeded to talk about every place we had to go in the recovery movement. She focused on racism and sexism and homophobia and adultism and able-body-ism and all the other 'isms and phobias. "We have to get political. And we have to get political in the truest sense, in the human sense."

David: That's great.

NOTES

1. Patrick Carnes, Ph.D., **Out of the Shadows,** CompCare Publishers, Minneapolis, 1983.

   Patrick Carnes, Ph.D., **Don't Call It Love,** Bantam, New York, 1991.

2. Mike Lew, **Victims No Longer: Men Recovering from Incest and Other Sexual Child Abuse,** Harper & Row, New York, 1990.

3. Held in November 1990, in Tucson, Arizona.

4. Laura Davis, with Ellen Bass, **The Courage to Heal,** Harper & Row, New York, 1988.

5. John Bradshaw, **Healing The Shame That Binds You,** Health Communications, Inc., Deerfield Beach, FL, 1988.

6. Men: Relationships and Co-Dependency, U.S. Journal Training, Phoenix, AZ, April 1990.

7. Safer Society Press, RR #1, Box 24B, Orwell, VT 05760.

PAT MELLODY

PAT MELLODY

Pat Mellody is in many respects the senior man in this group of six who were willing to share their views about recovery and the conscious man's movement. He is the executive administrator of ARC, The Meadows in Wickenburg, Arizona, and the husband of Pia Mellody. In both capacities, he has since 1978 supported and facilitated the recovery of an enormous number of people.

He is a quiet man whose moral courage pervades all his actions. He has been in contact with recovery since his father was a patient of Dr. Bob (the co-founder of AA) in Akron, Ohio, in the early 1940s. His own recovery began when as an Air Force officer he was put in charge of a base-level program dealing with social problems. In that capacity in the early '70s he enlisted the aid of Father Martin to start a 12-Step program, and after a while he recognized his own problem and got into recovery.

In his last year in the Air Force he was put in charge of six base-level social action programs. In order to facilitate this work he went to the Johnson Institute in Minneapolis where he met Vernon Johnson and Sharon Wegscheider-Cruse, among other members of the "Johnson Five." He also did workshops with Terry Kellogg, whom he later invited to Arizona to give a more "holistic" thrust to the treatment program there.

His work with Pia's recovery has had a large, although apparently indirect effect on the development of the theory and treatment for co-dependency. He has been a figure behind the scenes who, nonetheless, has exerted a strong influence in the evolution of work with co-dependency.

Our interview was conducted in his office, which is full of pictures of his children, his wife and his friends. In other times you might have expected him to be smoking a pipe. He also has a whole collection of souvenirs related to flying, which is still a strong avocation for him. His office gives the sense of being the still, calm center in the midst of a storm of activity and concern.

There is a sense of serenity in talking with Pat in this environment that emerges from his recovery. His sense of humor, his balance, his presence, and most of all his quiet irony reminded me of Mark Twain as we talked about issues of gender, co-dependency and the direction for the human race.

INTERVIEW WITH
PAT MELLODY

June 14, 1990 • Wickenburg, Arizona

David Lenfest: I'm very interested in your experience as a person who has been involved with addiction recovery for a long time and with the 12 Steps. Maybe you could start by giving me a five-minute vest pocket history of your involvement with the program.

James Patrick Mellody, a.k.a. Pat: My own recovery? Well, I guess my first contact with 12-Step programs was in 1945 when my father was involved in early Alcoholics Anonymous meetings in Akron. He was put in the hospital by Dr. Bob and he met Bill W.[1] He could have been one of the early people in AA except he only went to about five meetings. And he never drank again.

I used to say early in my career that he set a world's record for a dry drunk. But, in looking

at what we know now, the reality is that he was a very
severe co-dependent who suffered extreme emotional
child abuse. In his family of origin he was the only one of
seven children to survive to puberty. The rest of them
died of malnutrition and neglect.

David: Was that in this country?

Pat: It was in Pittsburgh of two alcoholic parents. Everyone on my father's side of the family that I know of
who lived to adulthood then died from alcoholism, except
my father. So part of that experience of growing up with
him was having a very bright mother who taught me,
actively taught me, how to think. It was the beginning of
who I am and the beginning of my looking at how recovery works both for myself and for other people.

My own recovery started in the Air Force. I spent a
career in the Air Force and retired as a Lieutenant Colonel
12 years ago.

David: Were you a pilot?

Pat: I was a navigator. Washed out of pilot training.
That's part of why I have a pilot's license now. I had to go
back and do it.

Anyway, I first got into not drinking because I got into
being a health nut in about 1967 or '68. I met a fellow in
the Air Force who was much older than I was and who
was in tremendous physical shape. We were flying the
Pacific in C-124s, low, slow, dirty airplanes. We'd land
someplace like Wake Island, and he'd go out and run ten
miles and I could hardly drag off the airplane. So I started
to talk to him about why he was that way, and he got me
interested in reading Adelle Davis [2], and, like everything
else in my life, I got fanatical about it.

But I quit drinking and went for about three years without drinking at all. Then I went to Thailand and spent a
year over there. I was lonely and miserable and convinced
myself that if I was going to hang around the bars because

that was the only place to be on the base, the least I could do was have a beer with my friends. So the last six months I was drunk a good bit of the time. I came home from there in August of '70 and moved to Tacoma, Washington.

I was going along drinking occasionally. My pattern never was to be a heavy drinker, except when I was in Thailand. There were very few times in my career when I drank an awful lot. It was more that it was unpredictable whether I'd drink a little bit or a lot. I couldn't accurately say when I went out and drank whether I'd go home or not. Or stay and drink till everybody else went home and then go home drunk.

Anyway, I was at a New Year's Eve party and it was a bring-your-own-bottle party, and we didn't know that. I was embarrassed, and I said, "That shit will never embarrass me again." And I never took another drink. That's a thing about me. I do almost anything well as long as I do it fanatically. Until recently, I've never been able to let moderation creep into my life.

David: I was going to ask that, because I remember from one of Pia's tapes that her definition of co-dependency is "a disease of immoderation."

Pat: Right. That's my stuff. That's my idea. You see, Pia and I have a really neat relationship as far as her work goes because a lot of her ideas are our ideas that we think of together. And so a lot of her boundary things, the emotional boundaries concept, for instance, comes out of how my mother taught me to defend myself emotionally from the Catholic nuns.

Well, anyway, I got grounded for some sinus problems from flying high altitudes and got into a new program in the Air Force called Social Actions, which was drugs and alcohol, race problems and equal opportunity in treatment for military personnel. I got involved at that time with a major who was interested in setting up a base-level program. He was a real go-getter kind of guy, and he organized a base-level alcohol program. As part of

that he got Father Martin[3] to come up and do week-long
workshops on the base. Another time he had William
Glasser, the author of *Reality Therapy*[4], come up and do a
week-long workshop.

As we got involved in doing things with treatment, we
were going up to a place called Alcenas up in Kirkland,
Washington, with Jim Milam[5] who's got a couple of books
out. I was starting to learn about alcoholism and treatment. I remember I started to look at my own drinking
and my own life, and I started to see symptoms there. I
had not been drinking for 14 months, and I was not looking at myself as an alcoholic. I remember talking to Father
Martin, and I said, "I was just wondering if I might be
alcoholic and if I shouldn't start a recovery program." And
he said, "We've been waiting for you." So I started in my
recovery program.

David: That would have been in the early '70s when
you first got into recovery. How did you make the shift
into The Meadows and into addiction recovery?

Pat: I was working in this base-level program and I got
transferred to Ohio and was put at major command level.
So I was in AFLC (Air Force Logistics and Command), I
was Assistant for Social Actions for AFLC, and I had six
base-level programs that I supervised. I was thinking
about retiring, and a guy from personnel came to me and
said, "We've been thinking about trying to do something
with the alcoholic civilians in the Air Force. If we gave you
$65,000 to contract with the Johnson Institute[6], would
you like to try that?" And I said, "Sure. I was going to
retire, but I'll give you another year. For $65,000 to play
with, I'll give you another year."

So I went up and met with the Johnson Institute. We
set up some training. At that time, the original founders
of the Johnson Institute were there, people like Vern Johnson who wrote *I'll Quit Tomorrow*[7]. There were several of
the original "Johnson Institute Five," as they called them.
Sharon Wegscheider-Cruse[8] was there. And so I got into

doing some work with Sharon. She and I traveled and did some work on Air Force bases with some of the other people up there.

When I retired, a friend of mine up there called and said, "Since you're retiring, (I was getting divorced again from my second marriage) why don't you come up and do an internship?" So I went up and did an internship, and about the third week I was there I was introduced to the people who owned The Meadows. I was hired almost immediately to come down here and be the senior counselor. I started in the Johnson Institute in October, and I came down to Wickenburg in early December as senior counselor and assistant director. I became executive director in six months.

David: This is '78? At that time, The Meadows was doing what? Drug and alcohol . . .

Pat: We were doing drug and alcohol treatment, although we were taking a few patients for what they were calling mental and nervous disorders, which we now call co-dependency. My view of treatment even then was very holistic. I understood that alcoholism is a primary disease, but I also saw that people had lots of other problems in life and that by focusing on just the alcohol we missed a lot. So at The Meadows we never held short of talking about anything. I used to be challenged about talking about incest and child abuse, all these other addictions and all these other issues that go on in peoples' lives. It's my view that although alcoholism is a primary disease, in order for people to recover they need to look at their whole lives.

It's easy to get out of one addiction into another one. So we started looking at all those kinds of things right from when I first got here. A different corporation owned it then. It was called Park View. There was a guy with Park View who thought I was unethical talking about these other things. One time I said to him, "You know, once it was decided I was alcoholic and couldn't drink any more, there wasn't much more to say on the subject." (Laughter.) "Everything else is treating the rest of how you live."

David: Yeah, and "the rest of how you live" is still dysfunctional once you've got the alcohol out of the picture. This question comes from my own curiosity or ignorance or both. At what point did the term co-dependency arise?

Pat: I think co-dependency — I've told enough people it's probably going to become a historical fact — my guess is that the word co-dependency came out of a book written in 1958 called *The Alcoholic in Your life* by Jo Coudert[9]. In that book she talked about herself as being the co-alcoholic, and I think the issue, co-dependency, came from the time when we got into "chemical dependency." It went from being co-alcoholic to being co-dependent. The inference is that somehow living with a drunk, with someone who was dependent, makes you a co-dependent. I think it's a very poor name for the disease. My belief is that co-dependency comes out of a malformed or poorly formed ego system from childhood in which my messages about myself are false. And that's where Pia says it's a disease of immaturity. We never developed maturity in our own selves, in our own ego systems.

David: Well, that brings us around to some of the Bly stuff. One of the things Bly argues is that a lot of our daily lives as men is a response to grief of different kinds and that we experience grief as wounds that are suffered in childhood and carried forward into adult life and not resolved. I wondered how you feel about that?

Pat: It sounds like the same things Pia and I say using slightly different words, using the word "grief" instead of childhood trauma issues or abuse issues. You know, I'm more of a politician than Pia is, and so I try not to say things that inflame people because when they get inflamed, they stop listening to what else I have to say.

So Pia and I have had discussions over this whole issue of saying co-dependency is caused by child abuse, which it is. But I prefer to say "co-dependency results from growing up in a family that was less than nurturing." And then to say, "In our way of believing, when a family stops being nurturing it starts being abusive." And what happens to the child depends on the nature of, the severity of or the frequency of the feelings going on around the abuse.

David: I was listening to a tape of Terry Kellogg's, and I was interested to hear him say that he thought the ideal environment for a child to grow up in was one of benign neglect in which the parents actually had a good relationship with each other and created and modeled good behavior for the kid and took care of the kid's basic needs and let them grow up. But trying to instruct the kid all the time, in Terry's image, was like trying to drive a car with the horn.

Pat: Well, I've never heard Terry say that, but I have heard Terry say that the hardest kind of abuse to treat is benign neglect. And that's what I say. Benign neglect is very abusive. The trouble with that kind of neglect is that statements about it, responses about it from a patient start with a *caveat*, "Well, he never, he just didn't." And that language talks more about the loneliness of childhood.

I think there are several reasons why we don't remember our childhood. Sometimes we don't remember our childhood because it was so traumatic. Sometimes we don't remember our childhood because it was plain vanilla. It's like going out into the Sahara desert and trying to find landmarks. There's nothing memorable that happened in childhood.

David: I'm trying to make distinctions between what happens to men as boys in childhood in contrast to what happens to women as girls. Or how we experience that differently as men. What is, finally, a man's path?

One of the images that Bly constantly brings up is the image of man as a hunter, and he tends to prefer a lot of the old Scandinavian mythic notions of the hunter. He prefers those over any image of man as a social animal or as a gatherer or finally on the bottom end of the scale as a herd animal at all. I wonder how you feel about that distinction, say, between hunters and gatherers?

Pat: Well, I don't know if I think in those terms about it. I majored in biology in college, and I look on man as a species first and then often try to look at what is species-specific about this animal.

A book I really liked years ago was *The Naked Ape* by Desmond Morris[10], in which he looked upon man as a biological specimen. What would you have if you found this species, a dead specimen of this species, and you took it into the laboratory to examine? What would you have here? He described it anatomically and then said, "What you have here obviously is a naked ape, hairless." (Chuckles.)

I think a lot that way. What is the species about? We're trying to talk in a sociological context about an animal that really has not been a social animal for a great many years. When we hear people talk about work addiction and the need to vacation and all those things, they are all brand-new concepts. The whole concept of vacation is new. People seem to think that anybody who works over 40 hours a week is a work addict. The 40-hour week wasn't developed by God, it was developed by Henry Ford.

David: Well, it was developed in opposition to Henry Ford.

Pat: No, it wasn't really. Henry Ford wanted a 40-hour week because you can put three eight-hour days in a 24-hour period, and you can run three shifts a day. Goodyear went him one further and found you can put in four six-hour shifts. So the rubber workers had what they thought was a major coup when they went to a six-hour day. Goodyear found it was more efficient to run four six-hour days doing boring work than it was to run three eights.

David: There isn't much of being a hunter when you're working on the line for Henry, is there?

Pat: No. I think we look for ways to have that kind of excitement, whether it's the hunter or the killer, you know. Desmond Morris or Robert Ardrey, one of them, talks about this species being the killer ape. Robert Ardrey, whom I like a lot, said, "Man became civilized when he stopped killing animals for food, and started killing each other for fun."[11]

David: Is he being serious at that point, or is he being humorous?

Pat: Both. He's being facetious, saying that we are a killer species and that we're not really the genteel people that we'd like to pretend we are.

David: Well, no, we're the only species that creates war.

Pat: I don't know. Ants do, species of ants do. There are other species that have wars. But our attraction to violence is so great. You know, spectator sports are about modified warfare.

David: What else is a football game?

Pat: Football games, fencing, it's about domination of one person over another, whether it be about killing or just showing up as being more agile or brighter. But it's always competition. We are a very, very competitive animal.

David: Do you think in this respect that men are more competitive, or how are they differently competitive than women?

Pat: It's becoming a mish-mash now, because there used to be really clear-cut men's roles and women's roles. A lot of that has been muddied by the fact that there are very, very few things a man can do that a woman can't do now based on the technological assistance there to do anything.

David: Well, and on social roles, too. For example, publishing is dominated by women these days.

Pat: Counseling is, too. I think teaching still is dominated by women. It used to be that school teaching was almost entirely a woman's profession, except in prep schools, and that the only male teachers were administrators or on a college level.

There aren't any clear lines any more. I don't think we can know what's biological and what's sociological.

David: What's nature and what's nurture? I think there are what appear to be mistakes. One of my favorite sort of anthropological writers was and still is Loren Eiseley[12]. There's a wonderful story Eiseley tells about a group of apes that were forced out of a gradually thinning forest and down onto the plains. Those were the apes that were forced to stand up, and they became our ancestors. The ones who won that particular war stayed in the trees, and they're still in the trees. We're the descendants of the ones who lost that battle, but who then were forced to adapt as a consequence. Eiseley finds that humorous on a cosmic level, and I do, too.

Pat: I grew up pretty isolated. I was sick as a child. I spent a couple of years with osteomyelitis. I had a lot of catching up to do, which I probably didn't do until I was in my 40s.

I grew up with women more than with men. I sometimes still relate to women a lot easier than I do to men. I may not be a good example of how to grow up in a man's world, because I didn't. I grew up somewhat over-protected. I never played team sports at all. My competition was like ping-pong, which I was very good at. I was very good on a bicycle. I could do things on a bicycle most people couldn't do. Probably I was a very competent driver, except the kind of driving I was doing should have been done on a race track, and I had lots of accidents. I think I got into proving my virility or manhood or something by taking risks with automobiles.

David: I did a bunch of that, too. I share that with you. I have often wondered in my own history whether that wasn't a semi-suicidal response to the child abuse in my background, which I was acting out by deliberately being out there on a ragged edge. Of course, in a lot of initiation rituals there is danger.

Pat: Probably the only initiation thing I went through was Boy Scout initiation.

David: You don't think of going to college, joining the Air Force, moving up through the ranks in the Air Force or that kind of thing as a male initiation process?

Pat: Right. I guess I had never considered much about being initiated into manhood. I was a very inadequate person for a long time in the Air Force. I was an officer and afraid of being an officer. I didn't like being saluted, didn't feel like I deserved it. Co-dependency issues. (Laughter.) Facetiously, I talked about running around the Air Force as a 14-year-old major.

There was a lot of truth in that. I was very, very emotionally immature at that time. What happened to me was in 1960 I was assigned to Griffiss Air Force Base in SAC (Strategic Air Command), and I started to hang around with a guy named Joe Drach who changed my life. He recognized that I was very bright, recognized my ability as a navigator, asked me to be on his crew, eventually got me a job as a navigator for a four-star general. Taught me a lot about how to be. Taught me a lot of dysfunctional ways of how to be, too, because we drank a lot together. That was where my self-worth started. In '59 and '60 I was 27. That was the beginning of my starting to like myself some.

David: I think it's very interesting that you're bringing together your experience in the Air Force at that age of

27 when the question started out to be initiation, and you came around to self-worth. So that for you the process of initiation was one of realizing your own self-worth. That in itself is insightful.

I imagine that will be true for a lot of people, and in fact that fits with the tribal culture, too. It's a way for the younger male to begin to value his own male experience through revering the senior members of the tribe. That's a little more obvious how that works. Although there you are, if you're being a navigator for a four-star general and you're 27 years old and you're flying around in a converted C-130. (*Pat:* C-118, plushest airplane in the Air Force.)

I'd like to go back to your experience with the Johnson Institute. A couple of years before that you had worked with Father Martin, and I don't know who Father Martin is.

Pat: "Chalk Talk?" He's a very famous priest in the field of alcoholism, and he has a treatment center he started called Ashleigh. He did some movies, *Chalk Talk on Alcoholism, Guidelines*, pretty famous. You can pick up almost any periodical, probably *Sober Times* has an article or an advertisement for his stuff. He started out with the Navy, working with Joe Purch down at Long Beach when Joe was still in the Navy.

David: Did you feel at that point that was a direction you wanted to go, working in the recovery field?

Pat: I really liked it. I always enjoyed working with people, talking to people. In the Air Force I did a lot of (Inspector General) work that was kind of having the airmen come in who needed somebody to talk to, and I'd be the one they talked to. I wasn't officially the IG, but I did the work for the guy who was.

David: You were his front man?

Pat: I was the wing executive officer, and the IG was the Vice Commander. I liked doing it and he didn't, so . . .

David: From my experience in the military, I always remember the IG with great fear and trembling.

Pat: That's a different thing. There's the base IG, and there's the IG at Air Force level that comes in and inspects everything.

David: Down to the very last paper clip.

Was your movement into recovery work in any sense connected with your sense of self-worth? Or did you just sort of fall into that as the next career after the Air Force?

Pat: No, I really liked it. When I first started getting into groups, Terry Kellogg was the first therapist I ever did any work with. He was doing work with the Johnson Institute. They had what they call a Learning Laboratory at the end of the three-week school. As part of the contract, I put myself through a three-week school to learn about alcoholism and addiction, and I spent about three days in pretty intensive therapy with Terry and a group of about eight people. That was really the beginning of my recovery from issues other than drinking.

That's when I see that I started to recover from co-dependency, when I really started to understand what was going on, understand some of the childhood issues.

David: And the systemic nature of addiction?

Pat: Out of that experience came the beginnings of a lot of my thinking about this. But also, my mother actively taught me to think and to challenge and to be skeptical and not to just take things as they were presented. Instead, to look at what's true about that one . . . I mean listen to people, what they really mean, not what they're saying. A lot of it came out of that, too.

So, anyway, I liked the work and when I did the internship at the Johnson Institute, I found I had a real flair for it. Ended up as an intern doing a lot of senior staff work. Came down here and became successful very, very rapidly.

I've always thought that God wanted me in, because I did absolutely nothing to get here. (Laughter.) I tried to leave once, and he beat me about the head and shoulders.

David: What do you think of these new gatherings of Wildmen that the Austin and Twin Cities Men's Centers are getting together and pound drums.

Pat: I haven't really heard a lot about it.

David: Is it necessary for men's recovery to go back into the past . . . I mean in everybody's recovery we go back and we sift through all that stuff at whatever age . . .

Pat: Necessary is a very strong word. It might be useful for some people. I don't think that everybody goes at all on the same path. I don't see myself as wanting to do that kind of thing. I do like backpacking. I haven't done a lot of it lately. I'd be someone who would rather take my sons, or my daughters if they wanted to go, and go out and just be in the woods. I don't need to make a lot of noise.

David: In these gatherings for men, a lot of male bonding goes on. A lot of the guys really enjoy that. They feel a sense of support and unity.

Pat: That's the same kind of thing we used to get when we went deer hunting together. I've done a lot of hunting but very little shooting. I've done a lot of tramping through the woods with people, getting tired and sitting around the campfire at night. The same thing is probably accomplished in the woods with the drumming.

David: A lot of men grow up around women who actively hate men. They experience some damage from that in the same way that women are damaged by men who hate women. There's equal damaging going on. One of the things I see happening with this new conscious man's movement is the rebuilding or the creating of avenues for men to respect themselves as men, and that's what I hear from a lot of men, too. For example, men who went to the Men, Relationships and Co-dependency Conference[13] in Phoenix shared that they really valued it because they were encouraged to respect themselves as men at that event.

Pat: One of the things that is really harmful to men and women is that so much of growing up takes place in front of the TV, which shows only people in extremes. Nobody wants to sit and watch a TV set showing moderation. (Laughter.) But for kids, it's difficult to separate reality from the facetious.

I remember in my second marriage, my wife's youngest son at age eight or nine could not understand that Fonzie in "Happy Days" was not a real person, and that some of these people who were really cartoon characters, actually a drawing, didn't really exist.

Look at all the double messages we have. This is a monogamous society in which everyone is supposed to be wildly sexual. You aren't supposed to feel pain. You aren't supposed to be anxious. The only way you can be adequate is to buy all these products. Advertising is about telling you that you're inadequate.

David: I think there's a similar kind of tricky message in older notions of what it was to be a man, "the code," for example. There was a code of honor with the Marines that was quite famous.

Pat: A friend of mine used to say, "The Marines aren't what they used to be, and they never were."

David: Nonetheless, there was this myth out there about being iron-jawed and being a great warrior and all that stuff. And for a lot of men that simply didn't fit. Did it work for you?

Pat: You're supposed to be ashamed to be afraid. See, to me, courage is not about not having fear. Courage is

about being able to act in spite of fear. So for me, it's okay
to be afraid. It's just not okay for fear to keep me from
performing.

David: Do you distinguish between a fear that has to do
with your perception of yourself and the fear you might
experience when you put your foot down and see there's
a rattlesnake? You feel afraid and you back away.

Pat: I'm not much afraid of rattlesnakes. I think fear is
fear. It's emotional fear. It's a reaction to a threatening
environment. What we feel as fear is really the body gear-
ing up to get ready. Slowing down, peristalsis, bringing
the blood in from the extremities, all that stuff.

David: Bly says you can't escape old habits without a
wound, and that whenever there's movement there's a
wound. How are these wounds different from the early
ones of childhood abuse and abandonment that people try
to medicate with addictions?

Pat: With one of them we're talking about our own
behavior, and the other we're talking about somebody
else's behavior. When we're reacting to the old wounds of
childhood, we're reacting to someone else's inappropriate
behavior toward us. When we're talking about moving
away from a behavior, you find out it's no longer a useful
behavior to you.

I can't remember the name of the guy from Minnesota
who wrote about self-defeating behaviors, and he says
the reason we stay in self-defeating behaviors is that we're
afraid not to. We're into a behavior because at the time we
developed it, it worked. Long after it quits working we
stay in a behavior because we don't know how not to.
We're afraid of trying an alternative, even though we
know this one doesn't work.

I think that may be what Bly's talking about in the
wound. It's the pain and the fear of trying something
different.

David: So in trying on this new image of manhood we're having to substitute a new sense of the role. Or he's suggesting we substitute a new sense of the role. It's one of my theories that most of us as men feel our roles to be so painful, so dreadful, in the way that we have been socialized into them and the things we have caved into as life roles, that we're ready to jump at change. Certainly, all the people I know in the program (CoDA and other 12-Step programs) are like that.

Pat: One of the problems is that as a species we don't have a way of recognizing needs that are being met. We only have ways of recognizing needs that aren't being met. If you sit down and study them, you can figure them out, but you don't have any automatic ways of recognizing a need being met.

David: You express satisfaction. Gee, that was a good meal. I really like my car, etc.

Pat: Okay, but those are momentary things. You don't hear somebody saying, "God, I haven't been thirsty all week. It used to be when I was younger I was thirsty all the time. Now I'm not so thirsty as I used to be." As long as that need for being thirsty is satisfied for the most part, it doesn't bother you any. The only need like that people worry about is the sexual need. They worry if they're not horny enough. (Laughter.) I tell them, "Why does it matter? If you're not horny, you're not horny. It's not an important thing."

Maslow, you know, in his concept of the hierarchy of needs[14] talks about "a satisfied need is not a motivator." I think that's the most important thing Maslow said. And so if you take that the next step, if the satisfied need is not a motivator, then the next step is that satisfying a need doesn't bring satisfaction. What it brings is a period of elation that you're talking about. That's a good meal, that kind of thing. But then going on, what other needs aren't being met?

I think we make mistakes in a lot of the areas in life in that we try to satisfy people's needs for them. All we do is satisfy this need and the next one is ready. What we really need to be doing is helping people to find a path to satisfy their own needs because in that process of working their way through and satisfying their own needs, they are developing self-esteem, feeling better about themselves and living and getting satisfaction out of the now.

Let me give you an example. I got divorced the first time because I didn't think my wife loved me, or that I was having romance in my life, or that my sex life was adequate, and so I left to find all those things. And I found them. When I found them, they became unimportant. I don't know if I found true love, but I found a good sex life, and it became unimportant. What happened then was all the rest of it crashed down on me. All those needs that were being met in my life no longer were being met.

I left seven kids and a seven-bedroom house on the hill up over Puget Sound, lots of friends and a support system and moved across the country into a small efficiency apartment. When I started realizing what I'd lost, I came very close to suicide. I didn't have a way to recognize the needs that were being met, and when they stopped being met they got me.

I think it's an important issue that we only have a way to recognize the needs that aren't being met. We need to look retrospectively at life often and look where we came from. Especially those of us who are recovering from co-dependency. We're so self-defeating. We look at the goal in our future. We set goals for ourselves, but they're nebulous things that can't be defined. And as we progress toward them, we redefine them. We always keep them in the future. Then we take our recovery and have this tendency to score it against this undefined goal. And we find ourselves in failure all the time.

David: Yeah. In one sense, being in recovery is boring because you have put aside or resolved all these things that were exciting.

Pat: We can learn to look retrospectively, with the help of a sponsor sometimes, at where we were last year. It's a "count your blessings" kind of thing. Look where you came from. Look at how much better things are than they were last year. You have a thorn in your foot, you pay attention to it. You take the thorn out of your foot and it feels better. It quits hurting. You don't spend the rest of the week taking joy in the fact that your foot doesn't hurt.

David: How does that recovery, that sense of moderation, interface or compare with a sense of competitiveness? With that thrust for . . .

Pat: Aging helps, but I think to deny that we're competitive is ridiculous. We're very competitive people. In my sense, when my kids play sports it's not very important to me if they win or not. It's more important whether they had a good time or not.

David: It's important to them whether they win or not.

Pat: It's important to their mother. It's important to the rest of the world if they won. I just don't happen to care. A lot of it seemed ridiculous to me. Team sports didn't make sense to me because I'm individually competitive, not a team player. And so I can be really excited about whether I can beat you at ping-pong. I couldn't get very excited at all if we were playing football if my team won or not.

David: That's okay. It's following the path. (Laughter.) Let me pick out another question because you're right, you're an elusive person. You're a wily character. Maybe your role is the trickster.

Pat: Could be.

David: Are you a trickster?

Pat: I don't know.

David: Do you see yourself that way sometimes — an initiator, a shaman? Are you a shaman sitting here running this outfit?

Pat: In some ways. I see myself as a thinker. I think I'm an innovative thinker. It seems to me that the way I think flies in the face of conventionality a lot.

Pia did a wonderful job of taking the whole thing and putting it together into something that was usable. I'm very concise. I say things in very few words. Pia can take the concepts and expand them so people understand them and work with them. It's a good union we have.

David: I'm also curious about the history of the movement. When did you guys get together, and when did you start . . .

Pat: Pia was here when I got here. She was head nurse at The Meadows.

David: That was '78?

Pat: Right.

David: That's very recent, that was only 12 years ago.

Pat: Right, the word really hadn't been coined yet, co-dependency. We weren't hearing it yet.

David: I've heard a lot of her tapes and profited from them enormously. They've helped as much as anything.

Pat: A lot of it came out of her recovery and her trying to work with her own childhood issues. She talks about that a lot. Terry Kellogg was mixed up in that, too, you know. We used to have Terry come down here and do workshops with the staff when I first got here. Pia and Terry and a bunch of us were together. Pia really got in touch with her childhood abuse issues then. That was the beginning of it. Then she went to treatment and got abused in treatment.

A lot of it is about looking at the bonds between people and the bonds between therapists and patients, priests and their parishioners, husbands and wives, and how the shaming process happens when you break those bonds.

David: Well, she's very clear about spiritual abuse. Both she and Terry are very clear about the connection between sexual abuse and spiritual abuse, how that can come together in the same person. That blew me out when I first heard it. When I first heard her tape on sex addiction and love addiction, I was so impressed with it that I actually transcribed it to try and get my hands on it.

Maybe we can talk about that a bit. As men we're presented with several kinds of roles that we can play, either the one of the constantly horny stud who is out there servicing females, the class II, class III sex addict out there functioning in the world, or we're the benevolent father or the work addict. Where's moderation in this? Is the program presenting us a model where this begins to come together, begins to be coherent?

Pat: Hopefully, in recovery we gain a sense of self, comfort with self. The primary relationship has to be with self before you can be in a relationship with anyone else. If I don't like me, how can I like you?

David: Is a man's 20th Century initiation really composed of grounding in the sorrow of the abandonment by his parents, his loss to and recovery from addictions and, finally, his re-emergence? In other words, isn't that finally the 20th Century American's process of initiation?

Pat: Maybe not initiation, but it's a process of what happens to a lot of us. (*David:* Of maturation?) Maturation, yeah. Initiation, to me, sounds like an external, formalized rite of some kind. I think what you're talking about is coming out of a dysfunctional family and eventually getting some recovery and some peace in life.

David: Well, there are any number of people, Wegscheider-Cruse and others, who say that 90 to 95% or more of the society is dysfunctional.

Pat: I always wonder where those statistics come from.

David: It seems that way. There are so many people around who are co-dependent or addicted to one substance or another or to work. We have that whole business about sick social institutions that Anne Wilson Schaef[15] wrote about.

That's why I've started to wonder if the process of maturation isn't the moving away from all of this into what, into moderation? Or into liking yourself?

Pat: I don't even know if we can use the term "maturation." We use these terms to talk about normative things, and the norm is so low. Who in the hell wants to be normal? Norm is a mathematical term talking about the average. Who would want to be an average of American life?

One of the problems, too, for us as men or as women is that we listen to people like Pia and Terry and Wegscheider-Cruse and all of them talk, and what they're talking about is things that are possible. What we do is we make that probable and move right into the imperative. And if we don't have these things, there's something terribly wrong with us.

To me, a lot of recovery is about acceptance. Although those things are possible in relationships, they're not likely. If they are likely . . . show me this couple walking around who has these things. I've been married three times. Terry is in the process of getting a divorce. Bradshaw just got divorced. Wegscheider-Cruse is on her third marriage. I mean, hell, who's got it? (Laughter.)

All of us running around. (Laughter.) Who are we describing? What we're talking about is philosophically what's possible. What people really need to look at is what's probable. I do a talk just for the hell of it once in a while for the patients, and I call it "Realistic Expectations." I do it on relationships. I get up there and say, "Give me a list of needs and wants that are possible to have in a relationship." I could say the same thing to you on your subject: "Give me a list of the needs and wants that are possible to the adult male."

So I write these things out on the board: "Fidelity, Truth, Maturity . . ." (*David:* Or you can go back to Maslow's pyramid.) You can get all of them. You can write them up there forever, "Unconditional Positive Regard, Justice." And I say, "Don't they look wonderful? Can anybody define any of them? How would you know when you had one?"

David: Sometimes we think we have positive regard for people. Of course, we never know if it's unconditional.

Pat: I don't think there is such a thing as unconditional anything. The notion of unconditional love is a goal, not a reality. I know I love my children, which is different from unconditional positive regard. (Laughter.) There are some times when it's okay for me not to like some of my children at all. That's the difference with love. I'd certainly do anything to help them through life, except destroy myself.

David: My guess is that you're hinting here at the distinction between the person and the action, that you might like the person but not care for their actions.

Pat: With people other than my children, it's a lot blurrier. When it gets further than my children, I don't try to divide whether I dislike somebody or their behavior, I just don't like them. I don't play mind games with myself to justify . . .

I think a lot of the things we say are good for explanation, but they don't happen in reality. It's like this drill people go through, "I know this is more about me than it is about you. I want to confront you about this. I don't expect you to change." When I do that with Pia, I know damn well it's about her, and I damn well want her to change. That's what's really going on inside of me.

You might stop to think about it. But when I'm angry with Pia, when I'm confronting her, I don't go through that whole drill, "I know this is more about me . . ." If that was about me, I would not be talking to her about it. So I think we get into what's philosophically probably correct, but trying to get it into daily life doesn't work very well.

David: That's really defining a philosophical struggle to make that code of behavior that we see in recovery realized, actualized in our daily behavior.

Pat: The reason that most people have trouble in recovery is they take things too seriously. If you look at it, there's almost nothing that matters. There's almost nothing that really, really matters much. Tell me something important, like the building's on fire and there's something between me and the door, or one of my kids is being abused. Now you're talking about something important. Almost everything else is kind of routine. We just get excited about things.

A lot of the problems we co-dependents have occur because we operate in extremes, we see things in extremes. We know other people's behavior is about us. I tried to explain that to Pia one time. I said, "You know, Pia, life's like a traffic jam. The reality is that we're all driving down the freeway trying to find our way into a smoother, faster lane. We know that's our motivation, and when we see somebody pass, cut across in front of us, we know that's about us." (Chuckles.)

David: Do you think a man's decision to face his addictions is made differently than a woman's?

Pat: I haven't any doubt of it. I think we have a different set of thought processes, a different threshold for various emotions than women have. We don't have that awful flushing of various hormones every month that women have that can affect their emotions.

My guess is that the decision-making processes are different, too, as much from a biological basis as from a sociological basis.

David: From your experience in this kind of work, would you say there is a typical pattern for men coming to face their addictions, coming to try to clean up that part of their lives?

Pat: I think women are a lot more eager and work longer in recovery around the co-dependency issues than men. When men clean up their alcoholism, they quit drinking and go to AA meetings, but they don't get as interested in the co-dependency stuff as easily as the women do. When men start getting fired up with it, they get interested, they get into it. I don't think they get into it as easily.

David: Why is that?

Pat: I think a lot if it comes out of "Big boys don't cry," and you're supposed to grit your teeth and stand it. Showing emotions is weakness. (*David:* Back to the code again?) Some of which may be biological, some hard to tell.

David: I think the code is largely sociological, largely nurture.

Pat: I think so, too. I think there probably are some biological things in there.

David: The answer I was expecting, what I would project on it from my own experience and from looking at other people, is that men who get into co-dependency recovery are the ones who look at the code and decide it doesn't work. "It doesn't keep me happy to have a stiff upper lip. I hate this job. I hate the whole way my life feels. I want to change that." And they're groping around.

Once they hit co-dependency recovery, they understand they've hit the emotional base that underlies the other stuff, and they're into paydirt. That's my notion about it, but you have this phenomenal experience. You've been running this outfit for 12 years.

Pat: I suppose. It doesn't make my experience any more valid than yours, broader I suppose.

David: What sort of range do you see?

Pat: I've had lots and lots of people go through here. The ones that end up in this office, the ones I get closest to, are the ones really having trouble with their treatment. And so my view of recovery and people is probably pretty jaded. Probably 80 to 85% of the people who go through this treatment program have very little contact with me. It's been a long month already this week.

David: What about shame? Aren't there aspects of the code that we're supposed to be? I'm using the code as a collective term to describe the John Wayne, stiff upper lip, the traditional male role models. It seems to me that it is based in shame, in counteracting shame.

Pat: I think that's true. I think we all have this belief that this code exists somehow. And none of us can beat it, match it. I think that's what Thoreau was talking about when he said, "Most men lead lives of quiet desperation." We all feel inadequate because the ill-defined code can't be met. So everyone is striving somehow to meet that, or to excel in some way to show that they're adequate.

David: Well, we come around to self-worth again, don't we? Is a man's self-worth defined by that code, or is it defined by a set of goals that he chases after? Or is it endemic to life? Bly, when he talks about the Jack and the Beanstalk myth, uses Bettleheim[16] and James Hillman[17], Hillman particularly, in interpreting it. He says one of the important messages of the Jack and the Beanstalk myth lies in the fact that he goes up the beanstalk at least three times, sometimes four times, depending on what version you look at.

And he grows each time he goes up. He gets more accomplished than he was before. And this is a definition of life. It's a constant chasing after one new goal after another. And I look at men who have multiple careers, as compared to our father's generation when traditionally a man would have one career, live in one house and retire. That would be it. You've had two. I've had three. We keep chasing up and down that beanstalk. So the question then is: is this personal, is this social, is this because of shame, is it shame-based?

Pat: Are you asking if ambition is shame-based?

David: That would be a question. Is one's ambition there simply to replace the shame core? Or to alleviate the negative effect of the shame core?

Pat: That's assuming everybody has a shame core?

David: Yes.

Pat: You see, I don't, I wouldn't think that would be true. I think competition is a natural thing. I think that we are a competitive species. If that wasn't true, if we weren't a competitive species, we ought to look at some place or some time or some culture where there was no competition.

David: Well, the Abo . . . would you say they have a competitive society, or not? They do compete with a brutal nature.

Pat: You don't think they compete to see who can throw the boomerang best, or hit the kangaroo at the farthest distance, or any of that?

I can't think of a culture in which there isn't competition. I can't think of a species in which there isn't competition. Really, I don't know if grass competes much except for space. Animals compete sexually. Women get into the same kind of posturing, sham battle stuff that men get into in some ways, don't they? If you can find the behavior or a close parallel to the behavior in other species, then I doubt it's based on a dysfunctional childhood.

David: So if our lives in that respect mimic the lives or careers of animals, then that says they're authentic?

Pat: I would think so, or at least the forerunners of it were authentic. I don't think competition has that much to do with overcoming shame. Because I think competition is inherent.

David: Can't you look at two competitors in a business or in a marathon, and one can be shame-based and the other not?

Pat: Sure. There can be different motivations for the same behavior. You may have someone who's getting perfect grades in school because they were held up in comparison to some other child in the family as lacking because this other child did better, and they decided they wouldn't let that happen to them again. And so they compete academically, not for the excellence of being academic, but to match up to their mother or father's expectations. But there are other people who compete academically just for the joy of competing academically.

David: I think there are a lot of people who would challenge that statement. I'm not sure I would, but . . .

This gets us around to independence. I get the sense as we talk that you're a very independent person. You take a very independent stance about things, and there are a lot of men, particularly men who come here for treatment,

who aren't able to do that, for whom that kind of independence would be impossible.

Pat: Well, not impossible, but maybe impossible at the
moment. I'm not even saying there's a real advantage to
independence. It just works for me. I'm not a herd animal.
I think there are a lot of herd animals in this species. I
claim eccentricity, because if you're known to be eccentric
you can get away with a hell of a lot. (Laughter.)

David: Do you think the urge to competition pushes us
into being "human doings" rather than human beings?

Pat: A friend of mine used to have a sign on his desk
that said, "Just because it's always been done that way is
not a reason to do it one more time."

David: So you get satisfaction from remaining a private
person, and Pia goes out and does all the front work.

Pat: I hear a lot of things that I thought of, or was part
of, in a lot of people's work. I like that. I like the idea that
the ideas are out there, that they're being accepted. I like it
that Pia's putting ideas out there that belong to both of us.

David: What are some of those ideas? Yours rather than
somebody else's? Whatever you feel comfortable talking
about.

Pat: A lot of the defining of co-dependency came from
here, came from Pia and me. I really can't separate what's
mine from other people's at all. I don't really try too much.
A lot of things like the origins of co-dependency, operating
in the extremes, things like that are things that we developed. All the issues around the core of the disease. A lot
of it came out of how the disease operates, Pia and I
having arguments, fights, about things. But defining it
into the five core issues and symptoms was Pia's work.
She really puts it in a usable form.

David: Was it generally out there that this disease comes from child abuse, or was that something that you put your finger on?

Pat: That's Pia's. That concept really came out of Pia, although there was somebody else that wrote from Switzerland who came up with the same kinds of concepts concurrently. The Zeitgeist . . .

Pia has this saying she uses a lot that I actually introduced her to that says, "Hug your demons or they'll bite you in the ass." She attributes the saying to me, but it actually came from Dick Cargill in Minnesota, which is where I heard it first.

I think a lot of worth and self-love comes out of facing your demons, facing and accepting your own humanity. I like what the AA Big Book says: "Strive for spiritual growth, not spiritual perfection." I think if we did that in all of our life, struggle for growth, not perfection, . . . Because when we have a goal that's finite, we believe it will be perfect, and then we focus on the goal. Really, the journey is the goal. It's about right now. It's not about what might come.

David: That's certainly true in all the mythic forms. It turns out that the journey becomes the goal itself. The path is the way.

Pat: To me, recovery is about being moderately comfortable on a daily basis. That's as good as it gets. And that's pretty damn good, as opposed to being terribly miserable on a daily basis.

David: I was interested to hear you say you thought you hit bottom when you moved to Ohio.

Pat: That was as bottom as I ever got. It was about a year later that I met Terry and got started in recovery. I had a guy who was my sponsor up in Ohio. He saved my life against my will. I met him about the second day I was there.

Actually, he worked for a base-level unit I was in charge of. He just took over my life. I was a Lieutenant Colonel and he was a civilian. He was at my door every night, and if I didn't have a damn good excuse I went to a meeting with him every night, every Sunday morning, too.

David: I think that's very important, your defining recovery as being moderately comfortable, in terms of the process, not a finite goal.

How about dignity? Where's dignity come into this?

Pat: I think dignity is about self-care, about self-love. It's about me feeling comfortable with myself and feeling comfortable in the world as myself. I don't think it's about being stodgy. It comes out of being respectful. I like some of the old-fashioned words like respect and honor and justice. I think I try to operate out of a sense of justice. I'm sensitive to that.

That's the Hippocratic oath, "First, we do no harm." That's really important to me. Whether we help somebody or not, at least we haven't hurt them.

David: Does that define justice for you, for the kind of therapy that goes on here?

Pat: I don't deliberately lie to people. That's important to me. I don't know if we talked much about a man's journey today. I don't know if I know much about a man, other than this man's journey.

David: Doing this book is part of my journey. Certainly, coming here was.

Pat: If you never print the book, you still gain a lot. That's another thing about success and failure. How do you define success and failure? If you can define you when you're a failure, you'd have to define you when you were successful.

David: We're back to Maslow's pyramid. Is there a bottom line success in being able to feed and clothe and house yourself?

Pat: I used to do aftercare. I did aftercare for years. This one fellow said as he was breaking up with his girl friend, "It's not the breaking up that bothers me as much as another failure." I said, "How do you know it's a failure?" He says, "Well, I'm not going to be with her any more." I said, "That makes all dating that doesn't end up in marriage a failure. Maybe you were in this relationship long enough to learn what you needed to learn in this relationship."

David: In closing, what observations do you have about man's journey, or do you want to sum up?

Pat: I think one of the problems is that I don't think very much in terms of one sex or the other. I think of it more as people's journey. I do a lot more work with women than I do with men as far as recovery. And I don't relate a lot to what is the man's journey in this country. I'm not interested in things that men are traditionally interested in.

David: Yet you go hunting and you hang out in the woods and you fly a plane.

Pat: It's a different kind of journey. I think a lot of that comes out of those important maturation years when I was sick as a child. Part of my abuse was that my mother really didn't make sure I had boys of my own age to play with in some crucial years. But I got to thinking that, as I said before, acceptance is a very, very important part of recovery. And I sometimes wonder if we don't, in searching, set the goals as unobtainable and think there's something missing in our lives if we haven't gone a particular path.

David: In other words, if we haven't got it fixed, then we're imperfect. Again, it's that notion of perfection getting in the way.

Pat: We may be out there desperately trying to fix it when a lot of it wasn't really broken.

David: That's an interesting position for you.

Pat: "Life is what you do until they close the lid." I enjoy life. I really love this job. I think one reason I'm fairly successful at it is that I don't take it very seriously.

NOTES

1. Bill W. and Dr. Bob were the founders of Alcoholics Anonymous (AA). See **Alcoholics Anonymous, the Story of How Many Thousands of Men and Women Have Recovered from Alcoholism;** Alcoholics Anonymous World Services, Inc., New York City, 1976.

2. Adelle Davis, **Let's Eat Right to Keep Fit,** Signet, New York, 1988.

3. Father Martin, **His Story,** American Audio and Tape Library, P.O. Box 64022, Phoenix, AZ 85082. See also **Chalk Talks in Alcohol,** Harper & Row, San Francisco, 1982.

4. William Glasser, **Reality Therapy.**

5. James Milam, Ph.D., and Katherine Ketcham, **Under the Influence,** Bantam, New York, 1981.

6. The Johnson Institute, 7151 Metro Blvd., Minneapolis, MN, 55435.

7. Vernon Johnson, **I'll Quit Tomorrow,** Harper & Row, New York, 1980.

8. Sharon Wegscheider-Cruse, President, Onsite Training and Consulting, Rapid City, SD, co-author **Understanding Co-dependency,** Health Communications, Inc., Deerfield Beach, FL, 1990.

9. Jo Coudert, **The Alcoholic in Your Life,** Warner, New York, 1972.

10. Desmond Morris, **The Naked Ape,** Dell, New York, 1980.

11. Robert Ardrey, **The Social Contract,** Macmillan, New York, 1970.

12. Loren Eiseley, **The Immense Journey,** Random House, New York, 1957.

13. "Men, Relationships and Co-dependency," Phoenix, AZ, April 1990, U.S. Journal/Health Communications, Inc.

14. Abraham Maslow, **Motivation and Personality,** Harper & Row, New York, 1970.

15. Anne Wilson Schaef, **When Society Becomes an Addict,** Harper & Row, New York, 1987.

16. Bruno Bettleheim, **The Uses of Enchantment,** Knopf, New York, 1976.

    Grimms' Tales for Young and Old. Tr. Ralph Mannheim, Doubleday, Garden City, NY, 1977.

17. James Hillman, **Puer Papers, Insearch,** and many other titles from Spring Publications, P.O. Box 222069, Dallas, TX 75222.

RESOURCE LIST

The following list is composed from references made in the course of the interviews. This list is intended to serve as a ready reference for the reader who wants to explore recovery and/or men's issues in more depth. For the most part, the list is arranged alphabetically by author, while some generic headings are included. In some cases, such as Bly's, authors have been grouped because of a common interest.

Robert Ackerman

"Perfect Daughters and Silent Sons: The Three 'I's' in Recovery (Isolation, Inadequacy and Intimacy)," Robert J. Ackerman, Second Annual Conference on Co-dependency, Scottsdale, AZ, August 27, 1990. Health Communications, Deerfield Beach, FL, 1990. Call (800) 851-9100.

Robert Ackerman, **Perfect Daughters,** Health Communications, Deerfield Beach, FL, 1990.

Alcoholism

Bill W. and Dr. Bob were the founders of Alcoholics Anonymous (AA). See **Alcoholics Anonymous,** the Story of How Many Thousands of Men and Women Have Recovered from Alcoholism; Alcoholics Anonymous World Services, Inc., Box 459, Grand Central Station, New York City, 10163, 1976.

For other information about the disease of alcoholism, these references were made in the course of the interviews in this book.

Father Martin, **His Story,** American Audio and Tape Library, P.O. Box 64022, Phoenix, AZ 85082. See also **Chalk Talks in Alcohol,** Harper & Row, San Francisco, 1982.

James Milam, Ph.D., and Katherine Ketcham, **Under the Influence,** Bantam, New York, 1981.

Vernon Johnson, **I'll Quit Tomorrow,** Harper & Row, New York, 1980.

The Johnson Institute, 7151 Metro Blvd., Minneapolis, MN, 55435.

Shepherd Bliss

Shepherd Bliss and the Sons of Orpheus may be contacted at P.O. Box 1133, Berkeley, CA 94701. Call (415) 549-1938.

Robert Bly

Robert Bly's books, pamphlets and tapes may be ordered from Ally Press Center, 524 Orleans St., St. Paul, MN 55107. Call (800) 729-3002.

Robert Bly, **Men and the Wound,** Minnesota Men's Conference, October 12, 1985. Human Development Association, Milwaukee, WI.

Additional tapes may be ordered from New Dimensions Radio, P.O. Box 410510, San Francisco, CA 94141. Call (415) 563-8899.

Keith Thompson's 1982 interview with Robert Bly can be found in **Challenge of the Heart: Love, Sex & Intimacy In Transition,** ed. John Welwood, Shambhala Press, Boston, 1985.

Bly prefers the following translation of the Grimm brothers. **Grimms' Tales for Young and Old.** Tr. Ralph Mannheim, Doubleday, Garden City, NY, 1977.

He also refers to this book (among others) for the impact of myth on children.

Bruno Bettleheim, **The Uses of Enchantment,** Knopf, New York, 1976.

For scholarly work on myth and Jungian theory, see Hillman and Moore.

John Bradshaw

John Bradshaw, **Healing The Shame That Binds You,** Health Communications, Inc., Deerfield Beach, FL, 1988.

Patrick Carnes

Patrick Carnes is most well known for his work on sex addiction.

Patrick Carnes, Ph.D., **Out of the Shadows,** CompCare Publishers, Minneapolis, 1983.

Patrick Carnes, Ph.D., **Don't Call It Love,** Bantam, New York, 1991.

Co-dependency

Information about CoDA (Co-Dependents Anonymous) can be obtained from The International Service Office, CoDA, P.O. Box 33577, Phoenix, AZ 85067. Call (602) 277-7991.

Thich Nhat Hanh

Thich Nhat Hanh, **The Practice of Mindfulness in Psychotherapy,** Sounds True Recordings, Boulder, CO, 1990. Call (303) 444-6229.

James Hillman

James Hillman, **Puer Papers, Insearch,** and many other titles from Spring Publications, P.O. Box 222069, Dallas, TX 75222.

Terry Kellogg

Terry Kellogg and Marvel Harrison, **Finding Balance, The 12 Priorities for Interdependence and Joyful Living,** Health Communications, Inc., Deerfield Beach, FL, 1991. See also **Changes,** January 1991.

Terry Kellogg with Marvel Harrison, **Broken Toys, Broken Dreams,** BRAT Publishing, 6 University Drive, Ste. 225, Amherst, MA, 1990. Call (800) 359-2728.

You may also contact BRAT Publishing for earlier tape series of Terry on the following subjects and others: Sexuality and Intimacy, Spirituality, Family Roles, Feelings and Physical Stress, Relationships and Shame.

John Lee

John Lee, **The Flying Boy,** Health Communications, Inc., Deerfield Beach, FL, 1989.

John Lee, **The Flying Boy II: The Journey Continues,** Health Communications, Inc., Deerfield Beach, FL, 1991.

John Lee, **Recovery, Plain and Simple,** Health Communications, Inc., Deerfield Beach, FL, 1990.

Information about John's tape series, his PEER (Primary, Emotional, Energy, Recovery) Training workshops, and his other lectures and workshops can be obtained from the Austin Men's Center, 1611 W. 6th Street, Austin, TX 78703. Information about **MAN!** magazine can be obtained from the same address. Call (512) 477-9599.

Mike Lew

Mike Lew, **Victims No Longer: Men Recovering from Incest and Other Sexual Child Abuse,** Harper & Row, New York, 1990.

Mike's treatment center is The Next Step Counseling and Training Center, 10 Langley Rd., Ste. 200, Newton Centre, MA 02159. Call (617) 332-6601.

Mellody Enterprises

For tapes by Pia Mellody, consult Mellody Enterprises, P.O. Box 1739, Wickenburg, Arizona 85358. See also Pia Mellody (with Andrea Wells Miller), **Facing Co-dependence** and **Breaking Free,** Harper & Row, New York, 1989.

Men's Conferences

Information about or tapes from the first (and subsequent) conference(s) on "Men, Relationships and Co-dependency," Phoenix, AZ, April 1990, can be obtained from Health Communications, Inc., 3201 S.W. 15th St., Deerfield Beach, FL, 33442-8190. Call (800) 851-9100.

Robert Moore

Robert Moore, a Jungian psychologist, may be heard on tapes from the C.G. Jung Institute of Chicago, 550 Callan Ave., Evanston, IL 60202.

Orion Foundation and Phoenix Consulting

Information about the Orion Foundation or Phoenix Consulting and Counseling can be obtained by writing to Ken and Mary Richardson at 321 W. Hatcher, Suite 108, Phoenix, AZ 85021. Call (602) 395-9959.

Safer Society Press

For the work of Faye Honey Knopp, contact Safer Society Press, RR #1, Box 24B, Orwell, VT 05760.

Anne Wilson Schaef

Anne Wilson Schaef, **When Society Becomes an Addict,** Harper & Row, New York, 1987. See also **The Addictive Organization** (with Diane Fassell).

Sharon Wegscheider-Cruse

Sharon Wegscheider-Cruse, President Onsite Training and Consulting, Rapid City, SD, co-author **Understanding Co-Dependency.** See also **Learning to Love Yourself,** Health Communications, Inc., Deerfield Beach, FL 1985.